Productivity,
Competitiveness,
Trade Performance
and Real Income:

Productivity, Competitiveness, Trade Performance and Real Income:

The Nexus Among Four Concepts

James R. Markusen

1992

ISBN 0-660-14683-5
DSS Catalogue No. EC22-190/1992E

Available in Canada through your local bookseller or by mail from:
Canada Communication Group — Publishing
Ottawa, Canada K1A 0S9

Publishing Co-ordination: Ampersand Communications Inc.
Cover Design: Brant Cowie/ArtPlus Limited
Translation into French: Société Gamma Inc.

Printed in Canada

Canadian Cataloguing in Publication Data

Markusen, James R., 1948-

Productivity, competitiveness, trade performance
and real income: the nexus among four concepts

      Issued also in French under title: Productivité,
      compétitivité, performance commerciale et revenu
      réel
      ISBN 0-660-14683-5
      DSS cat. no. EC22-190/1992E

      1. Industrial productivity -- Canada.
2. Competition, International. 3. Canada --
Industries -- Economic aspects. 4. Canada --
Manufactures -- Economic aspects. 5. Income --
Canada. I. Economic Council of Canada.
II. Title.

HC120.152M37 1992   338.6'.048'0971   C92-099749-X

Contents

Foreword

This is one of several studies commissioned by the Economic Council of Canada as part of a larger project on Competitiveness and Trade Performance. The project was designed to explore why Canadian industry has performed so poorly over the past 20 years and to compare Canada's performance with those of other industrial and newly industrialized nations. Studies show that Canada's position has been slipping relative to that of its trading partners, and that this jeopardizes future living standards. The project also provides valuable information about the feedback between the micro-world of management and labour and the macro-world of inflation and exchange rates. Its primary conclusion is that Canadians have not responded quickly or effectively enough to the challenges that have been taking place in international markets. The Council's findings were published in February, 1992 in a Statement titled *Pulling Together: Productivity, Innovation and Trade*.

Professor James Markusen was commissioned to do a conceptual study which would provide an overall organizing and integrating framework for the project. His study analyzes the determinants of, and the linkages and interactions among four key economic concepts: productivity, trade performance, real income, and competitiveness, using the competitive and the industrial organization models.

The author warns that one must be careful when using the term "competitiveness". There is little agreement among economists as to how it should be measured and how the resulting indicators, however measured, should be interpreted. Markusen advocates a definition of industry competitiveness based on total factor productivity (productive efficiency) which is a more reliable guide to real income than a definition based on trade performance. We have used this definition in our Statement. He adds that there is nothing "bad" about Canada losing competitiveness in low-wage, low-skill, labour-intensive manufacturing, although this does mean that the issue of adjustment costs must be addressed through public policy.

Professor Markusen emphasizes the need for caution with respect to industrial, trade and macro-economic policies, because certain changes to an economy are irreversible. However, he also argues that by pushing the economy along new, possibly diverging, development paths, decisions made by today's policy makers can have cumulative and long-lasting consequences for future productivity and real income. For example, a decision by government to give a domestic high-tech industry a head start over foreign competitors by providing financial support could give that industry a permanent advantage by allowing it to exploit economies of scale.

Because the Economic Council closed in June 1992, this study is being published by the Canada Communication Group.

James Markusen is a well-known specialist in international trade who has made important contributions to international trade theory. He is currently a member of the Department of Economics at the University of Colorado in Boulder.

Judith Maxwell
Chairman
The Economic Council of Canada

Introduction and Overview

Purpose and Scope

The purpose of this study is to analyze the interrelationships among four key economic concepts. Specifically, the analysis is an examination of the determinants of the relationships among and the interpretations of 1) productivity, 2) trade performance, 3) real income and, 4) competitiveness. The interrelationships among these concepts are considered from both theoretical and empirical perspectives and their implications — as they relate to public policy — are discussed.

In the sections following, general definitions are provided along with brief discussions. More detailed analysis is provided in subsequent chapters.

Productivity

A prerequisite for useful analysis is that all parties to an enquiry understand and agree upon the terms of reference and the subject matter under discussion. In the present context, this is not a simple matter. Definitions of at least one of the central concepts tend to waver and are often controversial. Even when there is general agreement on definitions, the question of measurement remains.

Beginning with productivity, there is not much controversy as to the definition of the term. Productivity relates to the level of output obtained from a given vector of inputs. Improvement in productivity is generally associated with underlying improvements in technology and in organizational efficiency. There are many arguments over specific measurement criteria and the construction and use of certain data (particularly capital stock data). Increasingly sophisticated techniques are being developed to refine empirical estimates, but almost all studies approach and define productivity in roughly similar ways.

The basic concept can be expressed with a relationship among output (X) produced from inputs labour (L), capital (K), and resources (R). The logarithmic formulation shown in (1.1) below is a simple relationship used to estimate productivity (1n denotes natural logs):

$$\ln X = \ln q + b\ln L + c\ln K + d\ln R \qquad (1.1)$$

If (b, c, and d) are simply factor shares in output, this essentially amounts to the assumption of an aggregate Cobb-Douglas technology.

$$X = qL^b K^c R^d \qquad (1.2)$$

In more sophisticated treatments (as in the translog formulations) second-order terms are introduced. (Price changes complicate the formulae, but more of that in the next chapter.) The parameter q in (1.1) is interpreted as the total factor productivity index, and the change in q over time is the change in productivity. Equation (1.2) shows that q is simply the Hicks-neutral technical change coefficient on the production function.

The difficulty with productivity lies not so much in its definition as with its interpretation. As is clear from (1.1), productivity is nearly always measured (rather than defined) as a residual after all other easily identifiable and measurable quantities have been accounted for. Since it is a residual, the productivity measure can be due to a wide range of phenomena. These include changes in the quality of the inputs (such as workers with high levels of education), mismeasurement of input levels (such as unobserved capacity utilization variations), misspecification of functional forms, and variations in scale when there are increasing returns in production (most studies impose constant returns to scale). With respect to scale, it should be noted that if the factor shares are defined to sum to one in either equation (1.1) or (1.2), then the researcher has imposed constant returns on the function.

None of these (four) causes has much to do with technical change or organizational efficiency. The point is that these variables or their proxies are absent in most studies and thus their effects tend to be lumped together with everything else in the empirical measure of "productivity". A clear indication that productivity indices are capturing considerably more than technical and organizational change is that negative values of q in (1.1) are often calculated. Since few economists accept the notion of negative technical change, it is obvious that the effects of scale and capacity-utilization are not only included in the productivity measure, but in some instances may even dominate it.

The problem with productivity, therefore, is that, even if everyone agrees on what it is, there still may not be a clear understanding of what is being measured.

Another complication is that productivity changes often carry normative (value) connotations that may or may not be justifiable. For example, is it "better" if real output increases because of an increase in productivity as opposed to an increase in the capital stock? If productivity increases are simply the effects of unmeasured increases in "knowledge capital" through investments in R&D or learning-by-doing, then this question cannot be answered without knowing the respective costs of the two types of investment.

Trade Performance

The concept of trade performance is related to a country's total exports versus total imports of goods and services and the relative changes in imports and exports over time. The term is used in a macro sense as a measurement of the (national) current account balance, and in the micro sense as a measurement of the import/export share(s) of individual goods and services. In the latter case, shares and ratios can be calculated across goods within a single country — as in the shares of different commodities expressed in terms of total Canadian imports/exports. Shares and ratios can also be calculated for individual goods across countries — as in the share of Canadian exports of good X expressed in terms of total world exports of X.

Certain indices focus on the share of a good in a country's exports relative to the share of that good in total world exports. For example, the Balassa measure for exports (discussed by Bimal Lodh in another ECC study) uses the following index to evaluate the exports of product i by country j.

$$(X_{ij} / X_j) / (X_{iw}/X_w) \tag{1.3}$$

where X_{ij} is country j's exports of product i, X_j is country j's total exports of all goods, X_{iw} is the total world exports (the combined total of exports of all countries) of good i and X_w is total world exports. This measure thus gives the share of the good in domestic country exports relative to the share of the good in total world exports. Alternative measures of trade performance are also discussed by Lodh in his study.

From (1.3), we see that there are two ways that trade performance in good i by country j can decline: the composition of trade in country j can shift, with the result that the export share of good i decreases; or because of an increase in similar share(s) elsewhere in the world.

It is also possible to focus on certain sectors in an absolute sense, such that the simple measure

$$X_{ij} / X_{iw} \tag{1.4}$$

is more appropriate. This expresses country j's share of exports of good i in relation to total world exports of i. (1.4) eliminates the ratio of total domestic to world exports found in (1.3). Comparing the two, we see that (1.4) could fall while (1.3) remains constant for either of two reasons. First, the world as a whole could be growing faster than country j or, second, country j could experience a current-account deficit such that its total exports fall relative to world totals. Neither macro effect will be picked up in (1.3). Which measure is the more appropriate depends entirely on the question being asked.

As with productivity analysis, the basic approach to trade performance measurement is not particularly controversial, but alternative indices are advocated and used. However, unlike the case of productivity analysis, there is a reasonable basis for confidence as to what is being measured.

The difficulties with trade performance derive from the interpretation of the indices. "Performance" has a normative or value connotation. Since the indices used are export shares, or export minus import shares, the notion of a "good" performance has a decidedly mercantilist flavour. Specifically, an improved trade performance is not necessarily related directly to real income and welfare. These points are considered in detail later in this study, but three quick examples are in order here. First, as noted above using (1.4), trade performance in a sector can decline if world population is growing relatively faster than the Canadian population. In such circumstances, Canadian exports in all sectors will fall relative to world totals.

Second, since shares must, by definition, sum to one, any change in a domestic economy will shift resources so that the total export (import) shares of some sectors must fall (rise). If, for example, new natural resources were to be found in Canada, some labour and capital would be shifted out of the manufacturing sector with the result that the total export (import) share of manufacturers would fall (rise). This should not be regarded as "bad", however, and in such circumstances the affected manufacturing sector(s) should not be branded as poor performers.

Third, there is some danger in using trade performance measures as indices of "revealed comparative advantage". While this may be valid in a perfectly competitive, distortion-free world, it is not a perfect measure in an imperfect world. For example, it is possible for a country to export almost any good if the production of that good is sufficiently subsidized. Such exports do not exhibit their comparative advantage except if the latter is defined in a tautological sense. However if comparative advantage is defined as those goods which a country ought to export in order to maximize real income, then subsidized exports do not reveal comparative advantage. At present, the quantitative importance of this problem is unknown.

In summary, similar measures of trade performance are in common use, and there are few serious measurement problems. There are difficulties, however, related to the interpretation and use of the measures — particularly with respect to their normative interpretations.

Real Income

As noted in the introduction to this chapter, real income is, perhaps, the best understood of the four economic concepts which are the object of this study. This is not to say, however, that real income is easy to measure. (Certainly there are economists who have devoted much of their careers to this issue.) In this sense, real income is like productivity; it is relatively easy to come up with an acceptable general definition but alternative indices, different econometric techniques and various ways of interpreting data leave the ongoing debate unresolved.

The caveats surrounding real income in an open economy point up the need for careful distinctions between the value of production and the value of consumption. The two are closely linked in a closed economy, but their relationship is more complex — and interesting — in an open economy. Part of the difficulty is attributable to writers (especially business journalists) who focus on production measures rather than consumption measures. In this respect, it should be noted that there are instances where the effects of a change on real income and the measure of trade performance (or production) of that change may have opposite signs (i.e., one may have a positive sign, the other, a negative sign). If we could get away with it, we would maximize real income by maximizing imports and minimizing exports, since the latter (exports) are a give away to foreigners. But we know that trade imbalances must be financed by the sale or purchase of assets and thus have implications for future consumption. With this qualification in mind, however, it is clear that we could increase our trade performance in a given period by measures that drastically cut our real consumption.

Competitiveness

The most difficult and controversial of the four economic concepts is competitiveness. There is little agreement as to its definition, how to measure it, or how to interpret the resulting indices, however measured. I do not propose — nor do I argue in favour of — a particular definition, nor do I have a simple or useful definition in my own mind. I would simply prefer to avoid the term, because it is a distraction from substantive analysis that is in no way dependent upon a single definition. In what follows, I will briefly review some of the ways in which the term "competitiveness" is used and attempt to interpret those implicit or explicit definitions.

The term "competitiveness" is used in ways that relate closely to all three of the concepts already identified: productivity, trade performance, and real income. In some cases, the use or application of the term is virtually identical to one of the other three. Consider first the relationship between productivity and competitiveness. Increases in productivity, unless accompanied by even larger increases in factor costs, are generally considered to increase the competitiveness of the relevant industry or country. Statements are made to the effect that "country j has a small, but highly competitive X sector". Thus, the sector may be only a minor exporter, but because it is profitable and healthy it is characterized as "competitive".

More often, competitiveness, particularly a change in competitiveness, is associated with trade performance. If, for example, country j loses export share in commodity X or import penetration in the X sector increases, it is said that country j is becoming "less competitive" with respect to X. Some economists would clearly prefer that the term "competitiveness" not be equated with trade performance, but the connection is often made, nevertheless. Researchers in public policy are at risk when they adopt definitions that differ from those used in the wider — national and international — debate. Competitiveness and trade performance are also often equated at the level of an entire country — with misleading results. Partly as a consequence of this practice, large current account deficits in the United States during the 1980s were often interpreted as a "loss of U.S. competitiveness".

Finally, competitiveness is frequently equated with real income. During the 1960s and '70s Britain was deemed to be losing competitiveness as its growth of per capita income lagged behind that of much of Western Europe. This general use of the term was applied to Britain during this period despite the fact that there were individual industries, such as automobile manufacturing, in which British firms were losing market share as well. The growth of competitiveness in the Far East is thought of in terms of rising income levels and current account surpluses. However, even if trade had been continually balanced, I believe that there would still be a tendency to refer to East Asian development in terms of "increased competitiveness".

The difficulty is not only with the multiplicity of (often implicit) definitions, but also with the fact that the definitions may conflict. As noted earlier, measures of trade balance for an industry or country may move in directions opposite to measures of real income. Hence, a notion of competitiveness based on one definition may generate results that are virtually opposite to those results produced by another definition.

As in the case of trade performance, part of the difficulty stems from the misuse of the term "competitiveness" as a normative concept and in failing to differentiate between the micro and macro applications of the term. The word "competitiveness" itself is also charged (at least in capitalist circles) with a particular bias; the implication is that more competitiveness is better. This may be a perfectly sensible concept and concern in the case of individual firms. Given an X industry, surely it is desirable that the firms involved in that industry be efficient (productive) and profitable, and able to secure market shares. Competitiveness at the firm level is therefore desirable. But this does not answer the question of whether the X industry is needed. With balanced trade, some industries will be exporters and others will be import competing. As noted earlier, any change in the domestic or the world environments will necessarily precipitate declining exports or increased imports in some sectors. Moreover, these shifts in response to the exogenous changes are deemed to be desirable.

Suppose that in Canada the X industry (i.e., the industry producing good X) is import competing and that industry Y is an exporter. Suppose further that world prices for Y's product increase and prices for X's product decrease, but that the net result is an overall improvement in Canada's terms of trade. I suggest that it is nonetheless legitimate to refer to the X sector in terms of a loss of competitiveness, provided that the term is not used in a normative sense. If we do the latter, then the inferred change in competitiveness (negative) is clearly at odds with a definition of competitiveness in terms of real income (positive).

One way to solve this problem is to make a clear distinction between the use of the term "competitiveness" in the strictly positive sense (as when a declining X industry is referred to as "losing competitiveness") and its use in a normative sense (in which case the X industry "losing competitiveness" may be desirable).

The tendency to equate trade performance with competitiveness is probably less controversial at the macro level that at the micro level of individual industries. If the country as a whole must run a current account deficit in order to maintain a real income level equal to that of its trading partners, then referring to that country "losing competitiveness" is probably valid in both the normative and the positive senses. But even here the normative interpretation is not completely clear. It depends on whether the capital inflow is being used for productive investment or to finance current consumption. In the former case, the current account deficit may be an investment in increased future competitiveness. Canadian industrial and resource sectors were built with such deficits (capital account surpluses). When the capital inflow is used to increase or maintain current consumption levels, the association of the deficit with losing competitiveness is clearly legitimate. From this perspective, the large deficits of the 1980s in the United States certainly seem to fall into the latter category.

Except for this one caveat, I am inclined to support a normative definition of macro competitiveness that focusses on real income relative to trading partners. That definition is closely related to one used by the Presidential Commission on Industrial Competitiveness in the United States:

> **Competitiveness: a Normative, Macro Definition** A country is competitive if it maintains a growth rate of real income equal to that of its trading partners in an environment of free and (long run) balanced trade.

For the purposes of this study it is still valuable to have a definition of industry competitiveness, even though it has only limited normative significance. General agreement that the definition is the most appropriate or useful is unlikely but it will at least be used consistently. However, a definition of industry competitiveness centred on trade performance will conflict with one centred more on productivity for at least three reasons, two of which have already been noted. First, if an economy increases its endowment of the resources used intensively in producing good Y, or the economy improves its technology in Y, factors of production will be transferred out of the X sector and into the Y sector, thus shrinking trade performance in X (increasing imports or decreasing exports) even though there has been no change in productivity in the X industry.

Second, a decrease in the world price of X due to new countries entering production will lower trade performance in X, even though productivity does not deteriorate relative to other producers. Indeed, in a world of increasing returns and imperfect competition, falling prices may well generate improvements in productivity. This is discussed in Chapter 3.

Third, import barriers or export subsidies may improve trade performance in a sector, but generally they do not increase productivity and, in the case of import barriers, generally reduce productivity in a world of increasing returns and imperfect competition.

I am thus inclined to use the term "competitiveness" in a way that is associated with an industry's productivity relative to that of other major trading countries. At the same time, I must point out how competitiveness changes if it is equated with trade performance. I use two alternative efficiency-based definitions.

Competitiveness: Positive, Efficiency-Based Micro (Industry) Definitions (1) An industry is competitive if it has a level of total factor productivity equal to or higher than that of its foreign competitors. (2) An industry is competitive if it has a level of unit (average) costs equal to or lower than that of its foreign competitors.

The first of these definitions focusses on technology and scale, relating physical outputs to inputs. The second definition focusses on costs, adding factor prices to the relationship between inputs and outputs. An industry can be competitive under the first definition, but not under the second, if it must pay higher prices for the factors it uses intensively relative to its competitors in other countries. Also, the first definition may have some normative content; the second surely does not. It is hardly "bad" that Canada is not competitive in unskilled, labour-intensive manufacturing. Also, by way of elaboration on these definitions: the loss of market share in a good due solely to the entry of new foreign competitors is not defined as decreased competitiveness, while loss of market share due to the increased productivity of foreign competitors is so defined.

It should be noted that competitiveness is popularly connected with trade performance. This is not particularly objectionable if, as noted earlier, care is taken not to endow such definitions with a normative connotation. Rather, the expression "losing competitiveness" should be used in the sense that the buggy-whip industry lost competitiveness early in this century.

Two alternative formulation also seem to be in general use.

Competitiveness: Positive, Trade-Based Industry Definitions In a free-trade environment: (1) An industry loses competitiveness if it has a declining share of total domestic exports or a rising share of total domestic imports deflated by the share of that good in total domestic production or consumption. (2) An industry loses competitiveness if it has a declining share of total world exports or rising share of total world imports of that good, deflated (divided by) the country's share of world trade.

The free-trade qualification avoids the problem of increased exports or reduced imports due respectively to export subsidies or import barriers. The deflator in the first definition solves the problem of generally declining industries (the buggy-whip example) when both exports and imports are falling because consumption is declining at home and abroad. The deflator in the second definition explicitly takes into account the problems of slower Canadian growth in population and the "catch up" in per capita income elsewhere. The second definition is essentially the same as (1.3) above. Even with these qualifications, it must be emphasized that these definitions have only limited normative significance for reasons outlined above.

I noted early in this section that the two definitions may often be in conflict. In the sections following I discuss other interesting cases where one definition follows the other in a time sequence. For example, in competitive models, a positive shock to an industry may increase its cost competitiveness in the short run. In the long run, output changes generate general-equilibrium effects (e.g., factor prices) so that costs are restored to the international level, but the long-run effect of the shock is manifest in increased competitiveness in the trade-performance sense.

Policy Considerations: Areas of Concern

As noted in the introduction to this chapter, the purpose of this study is to analyze the interrelationships among four key economic concepts. Ideally, a by-product of this analysis will be an understanding of the determinants of the four indices under discussion, and what a change in one implies about changes in the others. For example, when there are changes in productivity or competitiveness what, precisely, do these changes imply about changes in real income? This understanding, combined with the results of empirical work of the other studies commissioned by the ECC for this project is, in turn, a further input into policy analysis. It should help us to answer other key questions, such as whether decreased trade performance in a particular sector is, in fact, welfare-reducing. It should also help clarify our understanding of whether poor productivity in an industry is merely a result of inferior technology and poor management practices, or whether it is the result of a particular factor endowment or, perhaps, the result of small scale in a protected market. The analysis should also help readers understand whether or not productivity and competitiveness are being influenced by (existing) public policy, and which policies (e.g., domestic R&D policy versus foreign trade policy) are most relevant and appropriate. As part of the prelude to the policy analysis, we must determine what we should be worried about and what we can actually influence. For example, if Canada is observed to have a low and/or declining share of world trade in "high-tech" products, should we worry about this, or is it the efficient outcome of a changing world? And what, if anything, can or should be done about it, and by whom? I hope to be able to shed some light on these questions.

Framework of the Study

The following chapters are organized around alternative analytical models as well as around specific issues. This organization is intended to facilitate repeated use of a simple model without requiring the reader to understand other techniques. Chapter 2 develops and analyzes a simple competitive general-equilibrium model, examining the effects of changes in technology, factor endowments, and world prices on productivity, trade performance, and measures of real income. Government policies are then analyzed, and the roles of international capital mobility and endogenous capital accumulation are developed. The last section examines the theory put forward in the light of empirical evidence as to the relevance of the competitive model.

Chapter 3 takes an industrial-organization approach in which some industries have increasing returns to scale and imperfect competition. Determinants of firm scale are developed and related to productivity, competitiveness, and measures of trade performance. The role of key assumptions, such as the ease of entry and exit, are analyzed, as are the effects of both domestic and foreign trade barriers. The last section in the chapter reviews empirical evidence drawn from both factual and counterfactual studies, to determine the quantitative relevance of this approach and the appropriate structural assumptions.

Chapter 4 is devoted to the issues of R&D, learning, externalities, and spillovers. In considering these factors, there is no presumption that market outcomes are efficient — nor is there in the industrial organization model. The focus of the chapter therefore is how market failure creates a role for industrial and trade policy that differs markedly from the role suggested by competitive trade theory. The chapter then reviews empirical evidence to suggest the direction and quantitative importance of market failures. For example, is the social rate of return to investment in training or R&D significantly different from the private rate of return?

Finally, Chapter 5 provides a review and non-technical summary of the study, along with a number of references to Pulling Together, a statement published in 1992 by the Economic Council of Canada. Readers who are uninterested in technical details may wish to skip directly to that chapter.

The Competitive Model

The Basic Model and its Implications

U ntil about ten years ago, students of international trade were taught a single approach to trade theory based on the assumption that firms produce with constant returns to scale (CRS) and that market structures are perfectly competitive (PC) — hereafter referred to as the CRS/PC model. Within this general framework, textbooks presented two basic variations. The first, known as the Ricardian model, assumes that countries have exogenous differences in production technologies. The second, known as the factor-proportions model, assumes that countries have identical technologies but different relative factor endowments. Until 1980, most of the emphasis in trade theory was on the latter. Indeed, a very specific form was known as the Heckscher-Ohlin model, where there are exactly two goods and two factors, with both factors used in and mobile between the two industries.

This chapter reviews the CRS/PC model and its implications for the four key concepts introduced in the preceding chapter. But first, a sketch of the general outline of this approach is in order along with some references to its basic implications. (Subsequent sections will provide more detail about the underlying technology and structure.)

The production side of the CRS/PC model generates a production frontier between good X and good Y as shown by the curve TT' in Figure 2.1. The returns to scale in production are constant, but the frontier may be bowed out — as shown by the curve due to the effects of factor intensity (defined in the next section). Assume for the moment that there are no distortions in production. Constant returns together with perfect competition by producers then imply that, at a given set of prices, production will occur at a point of tangency between the production frontier and the price ratio (p_x / p_y). This notation is simplified throughout the chapter by using p to represent the price ratio p_x / p_y, or alternatively the price of X in terms of Y. A superscript on p

Figure 2.1

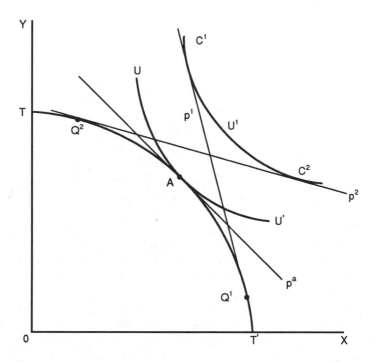

(e.g., p^1) denotes a specific value of $p = p_x / p_y$. The slope of the production frontier is generally referred to as the marginal rate of transformation (MRT).

Consumer demand is represented in the model by a field of community indifference curves in Figure 2.1 (e.g., UU'). Utility maximization by consumers (in the absence of distortions) implies a tangency between an indifference curve and the price ratio p, with the slope of an indifference curve referred to as the marginal rate of substitution (MRS). Autarky equilibrium for a country is determined by three conditions: (1) the producer equilibrium condition p = MRT, (2) the consumer equilibrium condition p = MRS, and (3) the market clearing condition that the supply and demand for each good are equal. If C_x and C_y are the consumption of X and Y respectively, this last condition is written as $X = C_x$ and $Y = C_y$.

An autarky equilibrium for the economy is shown at point A in Figure 2.1. Here an indifference curve and the production frontier are both tangent to the common equilibrium price ratio p^a. Since point A represents both the consumption point and the production point, markets clear. Note that the equilibrium involves the highest possible level of utility subject to the production constraint described by the production frontier. The CRS/PC model thus has the Smithian "invisible hand" — that free market equilibrium leads to an optimum.

Now suppose that the country can engage in trade at a price ratio that differs from the autarky price ratio. Two such price ratios are denoted p^1 and p^2 in Figure 2.1. The first two conditions for equilibrium listed above still apply: p^i = MRT = MRS. But market clearing is no longer necessary; that is, we are no longer constrained to consume only what we produce. In place of the market clearing, a balance of trade constraint can be imposed that can be expressed in either of two ways.

$$p\,(X - C_x) + (Y - C_y) = 0 \quad \text{or} \quad pX + Y = pC_x + C_y \qquad (2.1)$$

The first equation requires that the sum of the values of the excess supply of each of the two goods equals zero. A positive export of X is balanced by a negative export (import) of Y or vice versa. The second equation simply rearranges the terms, and states that the value of production equals the value of consumption at world prices. Note that if the left side of the first equation is negative (a balance of trade deficit) then the left side of the second equation is (quantitatively) less than the right side. Thus a balance of trade deficit can be seen to express the exact equivalent to the statement: "a country is consuming more than it is producing".

The equations in (2.1) imply that the world price ratio through the production point forms a "budget line" in the sense that consumers can pick any point on that budget line, since the values of consumption and production at world prices are equal and hence satisfy (2.1). Let Q denote a production point (X, Y) and C denote a consumption point (C_x, C_y). Superscripts (e.g., C^1) identify specific points. In Figure 2.1 producers and consumers choose points Q^1 and C^1 respectively when the price ratio is p^1, while they choose Q^2 and C^2 at price ratio p^2. (The diagram has been drawn so that the two consumption points lie on the same indifference curve in order to make a point to be discussed shortly.)

Several results can be seen in Figure 2.1.

• A country will gain from trade whenever it can trade at a price ratio that is different from its autarky price ratio.

• The direction of trade (import vs export) in a free trade equilibrium is determined by the difference between the world price ratio and the autarky price ratio. In the case of p^1, the relative world price of X is higher than the autarky price (pa) so the country exports X and imports Y. In the case of p^2, the relative world price of X is lower than the autarky price, so the country imports X and exports Y. Gains from trade are captured by exporting the good that is more valuable abroad than at home and importing the good from abroad that is relatively more costly to produced at home.

- If world prices are fixed, free trade is optimal. At price ratio p^1, for example, it is impossible for the country to do better than to obtain utility level U^1 if the balance-of-trade constraint is imposed. This is the Smithian "invisible hand" result extended to the open economy.
- There is no role for the government to play in increasing real income either by promoting exports or by restricting imports. (The latter relies on the assumption of fixed world prices while the former does not.) The undistorted, CRS/PC economy chooses precisely the right amount of imports and exports.
- There is no normative significance to the direction of trade. It is not "better" (or worse) to be an exporter (or an importer) of X or Y. The optimal direction of trade is determined by underlying conditions of supply and demand.
- There is no normative significance to which of the two sectors in Figure 2.1 is the high value-added sector. No information about intermediate use can be gleaned from the diagram — which is a net output frontier. The notion that "the government should encourage the expansion of high value-added sectors" is therefore irrelevant in this model.
- The resulting gains from trade shown in Figure 2.1 do not depend on the productivity level of the economy or on its competitiveness relative to its trading partner. This means that other countries (i.e. our trading partners) could have an "absolute advantage" in all goods, but our country would still gain from trade in general. Gains from trade, as first demonstrated by Ricardo, depend only on there being a difference in comparative advantage — which is here interpreted as the difference between the world price and the autarky price ratio. It is important to emphasize that even if a country is "uncompetitive" in the sense of the definition provided in Chapter 1, it can still gain from trade. The fact of a relative lack of competitiveness must not be used as a reason — a justification — either to restrict or to subsidize trade.

A Two-Good, Three-Factor Model

This section develops a simple model to illustrate the effects of internal and external changes on the economy. The model is a variation of the sector-specific-factors model, employing two goods: (X and Y), and three factors: labour (L), capital (K), and resources (R). The X sector uses labour and capital while the Y sector uses labour and resources. L_x and L_y denote the allocations of the total labour endowment (L) between the two sectors. The production functions are Cobb-Douglas, with an identical labour share (b) in each industry. q_x and q_y denote the Hicks-neutral technical efficiency coefficients in the two sectors. The production sector is expressed by:

$$X = q_x L_x{}^b K^{1-b} \tag{2.2}$$

$$Y = q_y L_y{}^b R^{1-b} \tag{2.3}$$

$$L = L_x + L_y \tag{2.4}$$

Constant returns to scale in both factors are exhibited by the production of X and Y, but marginal products of K and R diminish when more labour is added to a fixed factor.

These production functions depict a frontier of production possibilities such as that shown in Figure 2.1 by TT'. Beginning at T, the production of X can be increased and the production of Y can be decreased by shifting labour to the X sector. Since labour is added to a fixed factor in X, the marginal product of labour in X (MP_{1x}) falls as this process continues and the marginal product of labour rises in Y (MP_{1y}) since there are fewer and fewer units of labour to combine with the fixed resource stock. The slope of the production frontier (MRT) is given by the ratio of these marginal products.

$$- dY / dX = -(dY / dL_x) / (dX / dL_x) = (dY / dL_y) / (dX / dL_x)$$

$$= (MP_{1y}) / (MP_{1x}) \tag{2.5}$$

where the second equality follows from (2.4): $dL_x = -dLy$. As was just noted, the marginal product of labour in Y rises and that in X falls as one moves down the production frontier in Figure 2.1. Equation (2.5) establishes that the effect of diminishing marginal product implies that the production frontier becomes steeper as one moves from T to T' in Figure 2.1, hence the concave shape. Since the MRT is equal to the price ratio in general equilibrium, the result is that the general-equilibrium supply curves slope upward: a higher price for X generates a larger output of X and a smaller output of Y.

An important characteristic of this technology is that factor prices change as one moves around the production frontier. As was just noted, the movement from T to T' due to an increase in the relative price of X in Figure 2.1 is accomplished by transferring labour from Y to X. In competitive equilibrium, factor prices are given by the value of marginal products

$$w = p_x (MP_{1x}) = p_y (MP_{1y}) \tag{2.6}$$

$$r_x = p_x (MP_{kx}) \tag{2.7}$$

$$r_y = p_y (MP_{ry}) \tag{2.8}$$

where r_x and r_y are the returns to the specific factors K and R respectively, and s is the wage. Now, consider increasing p_x holding p_y constant. It has already been established that MP_{1y} rises while MP_{1x} falls. Equation (2.6) implies that w increases more than p_y (which is constant) but by less than p_x. In (2.7) MP_{kx} increases as more labour is added to the fixed capital stock and in (2.8)

MP_{ry} falls as less labour is combined with resources in Y. (2.7) and (2.8) then imply that r_x rises by more than p_x and r_y fall. Combining these results produces the income-redistribution effect of an increase in p_x, $dp_x > 0$.

$$dr_x / r_x > dp_x / p_x > dw / w > 0 > dr_y / r_y \qquad (2.9)$$

Owners of capital are absolutely better off; owners of resources are absolutely worse off; and labour gains in terms of good Y but loses in terms of good X. Labour's utility gain thus depends in part on the composition of its consumption bundle.

Trade will depend on the shares of X and Y in terms of total production relative to consumption. The relative shares of production in the model are expressed by:

$$(p_x X) / (p_y Y) = [(p_x q_x)^c K] / [(p_y q_y)^c R] \qquad (2.10)$$

where $c = 1 / (1-b) > 1$. Increases in p_x, q_x, or K increase the share of X in production.

The GNP function for this economy is defined as the maximum value of production at given prices.

$$GNP = maximum \{p_x X + p_y Y\} \qquad (2.11)$$

subject to (X,Y) on production frontier.

The GNP function for our economy takes the following form:

$$GNP = [(p_x q_x)^c K + (p_y q_y)^c R]^{1/c} L^b \qquad 1 / c = (1-b) \qquad (2.12)$$

Note that GNP is homogeneous of degree one in all endowments and homogeneous of degree one in prices. GNP is a constant-elasticity-of-transformation (CET) function of $(p_x q_x)$ and $(p_y q_y)$ with weights of K and R respectively. Note too the symmetric role of prices and the technical efficiency coefficients in determining GNP. The GNP function also allows output per worker (GNP/L) and the wage rate (the marginal product of labour) to be expressed solely in terms of the exogenous variables.

$$GNP / L = [(p_x q_x)^c K + (p_y q_y)^c R]^{1/c} L^{b-1} \qquad (2.13)$$

$$w = d (GNP) / dL = b[(p_x q_x)^c K + (p_y q_y)^c R]^{1/c} L^{b-1} \qquad (2.14)$$

The two equations imply a constant proportional relationship between w and GNP per worker: $w = b(GNP/L)$.

We now turn to the demand side of the general equilibrium model in order to determine real income and trade patterns.

Let the utility function take the simple Cobb-Douglas form with equal weights on X and Y.

$$U = C_x^{.5} C_y^{.5} \qquad (2.15)$$

Maximizing (2.15) subject to the budget constraint $GNP = p_xX + p_yY$ gives us the demand functions:

$$C_x = GNP / (2p_x), \; Cy = GNP / (2p_y) \tag{2.16}$$

Multiplying the demand functions by their respective prices, it can be seen that consumption shares are independent of prices and equal to one half.

$$p_xC_x / GNP = p_yC_y / GNP = 1/2. \tag{2.17}$$

Placing the demand functions back into the utility function generates the indirect utility function, where utility is a function of prices and the other exogenous variables.

$$U = GNP \, (1/2p_x)^{.5}(1/2p^y)^{.5} = GNP \, (p_xp_y)^{-.5}/2 \tag{2.18}$$

Substituting GNP into (2.18) produces an expression for real income (utility) as a function of exogenous variables only.

$$U = \{ \, [\, (p_xq_x)^cK + (p_yq_y)^cR]^{1/c}L^b\}(p_xp_y)^{-.5}/2 \tag{2.19}$$

The term $(p_xp_y)^{-.5}/2$ is thus the true "consumer price index" that deflates the change in nominal GNP to arrive at real income. Note that while prices and technical efficiency parameters enter symmetrically in determining nominal GNP, they do not do so in determining real income U.

Let P denote the population of the country and let (par) = L/P denote the labour force participation rate. Divide both sides of (2.19) by P. Real income per capita is then given by:

$$U/P = (par) \{ \, [\, (p_xq_x)^cK + (p_yq_y)^cR]_1^{/c}L^{b-1}\}(p_xp_y)^{-.5}/2 \tag{2.20}$$

Real income per capita increases unambiguously with q_x, q_y, K, R, and the participation rate, and decreases unambiguously with L. (The role of prices is ambiguous and is discussed later.) At constant world prices, GNP per worker, the wage rate, and real income per worker all move together.

This model also provides a simple expression for the direction of trade. The country exports X if — and only if — the share of X in total production exceeds the share of X in consumption. With reference to (2.10) and (2.17), we obtain:

$$[(p_xq_x)^cK] / [(p_yq_y)^cR] > 1 \text{ implies X is exported.} \tag{2.21}$$

The direction of trade is determined by world relative prices, the technical efficiency parameters, the relative levels of the two sector-specific factors, and the ratio of consumption shares (equal to one) reflecting preferences. The country will export X when 1) the world relative price of X is high, 2) the country is relatively technically efficient in X production, and 3) the country is relatively well-endowed with capital (i.e. the factor specific to X production).

The direction of trade does not depend on L in this model because both sectors are equally labour intensive. This is generally not the case, but the assumption of equal labour share in the two sectors is necessary in order to derive a closed form GNP function. It should be noted for future reference that either R or K can be considered as human capital which is combined with "raw" labour to produce skilled labour if there is a need to designate one of the sectors as human-capital intensive. The output of that sector, then, is simply a linear function of the supply of skilled labour.

Relating this model to the well-known Heckscher-Ohlin model (in which there are only two factors, with both factors used in both sectors), our model can be thought of as a short-run version of that model in which capital assumes a specific form that is not useful in the other sector. Over time, capital can be depreciated in one sector and created in the other, thus providing a long-run Heckscher-Ohlin model. The only difficulty is that the equal factor-intensity assumption implies a linear long-run production frontier and therefore specialization. However, if there is an increasing cost to transforming capital from one form to the other, then there is still a strictly concave long-run transformation function as will be discussed later.

An Index and an Example

Many indices have been proposed and used to measure real income and productivity change. To show how they work, I will explore a relatively sophisticated example derived by Diewert and Morrison (1986) and applied to Canadian data by Cas, Diewert, and Ostensoe (1986).

Let superscripts $(0,1)$ denote initial and final time periods respectively, and let GNP^0 and GNP^1 denote the GNP functions for the two time periods. Productivity changes are determined by evaluating these at a common price (p) and with an endowment vector $(V = [L, K, R])$. Based-weighted (Laspeyres) and final-weighted (Paasche) indices are then given by:

$$R_L = GNP^1(p^0, V^0) / GNP^0(p^0, V^0) \qquad (2.22)$$

$$R_P = GNP^1(p^1, V^1) / GNP^0(p^1, V^1) \qquad (2.23)$$

These indices show the increase in output at constant prices and endowments. Diewert and Morrison show that if GNP is translog and there is competitive, profit-maximizing behaviour, then the geometric mean of the two productivity indexes defined by (2.22) and (2.23) is precisely equal to the translog implicit output index divided by the translog input index for the two time periods. Let S^i_j be the share of good j in output in period i and let S^i_k be the share of factor k in output in period i. The Diewert/Morrison productivity index is then given by:

$$(R_L * R_p)^{1/2} = A/(BC) \tag{2.24}$$

where:

$$A = GNP^1 / GNP^0 = (p_x^1 X^1 + p_y^1 Y^1) / (p_x^0 X^0 + p_y^0 Y^0) \tag{2.25}$$

$$\ln B = (1/2) \{ [S_x^1 + S_x^0] \ln (p_x^1 / p_x^0) + [S_y^1 + S_y^0] \ln (p_y^1 / p_y^0) \} \tag{2.26}$$

$$\ln C = (1/2) \{ [S_l^1 + S_l^0] \ln (w^1 / w^0) + [S_k^1 + S_k^0] \ln (r_x^1 / r_x^0)$$

$$+[S_r^1 + S_r^0] \ln (r_y^1 / r_y^0) \} \tag{2.27}$$

A is thus the ratio of nominal GNP in the two periods. B is a price index (1/B is the price deflator) so A/B is an output index. C is the translog input index, so dividing by C removes the influence of endowment changes in the change in GNP. Therefore, the productivity index measures the change in GNP, holding prices and endowments constant.

Alternatively, A/B is the change in real GNP due to both productivity and endowment changes, so the change in real GNP (which we denote RGNP^1/RGNP^0) can be written as:

$$RGNP^1/RGNP^0 = [A/(BC)]_*[C] = [productivity]_*[endowment] \tag{2.28}$$

thus breaking the change in real GNP into productivity and factor endowment components.

Now consider Figure 2.2, which shows two price ratios p^1 and p^0. (2.28) provides a measure of the real GNP change in moving from p^0 to p^1. However, the diagram shows that the effect of this change on real income or utility clearly depends on which good is exported. If the initial consumption point is C^0 and there is a move to C^1, welfare clearly improves because the relative price of the export good has risen. But if the initial consumption point is $C^{0'}$ and there is a move to $C^{1'}$, then welfare deteriorates since the relative price of the import good has risen.

Accordingly, equation (2.28) is not an accurate measure of real income or utility. Diewert and Morrison deal with this problem by introducing a terms-of-trade index which is, again, the geometric mean of a Laspeyres and a Paasche index. Suppose X is the export good and Y is the import good, and let E_x and M_y denote the shares of exports and imports in GNP respectively. The Diewert/Morrison terms-of-trade index is then given by D/E, where:

$$\ln D = (1/2) [E_x^1 + E_x^0] \ln(p_x^1 / p_x^0) \tag{2.29}$$

$$\ln E = (1/2) (M_y^1 + M_y^0) \ln(p_y^1 / p_y^0) \tag{2.30}$$

The terms-of-trade index rises if the relative price of the export good X

Figure 2.2

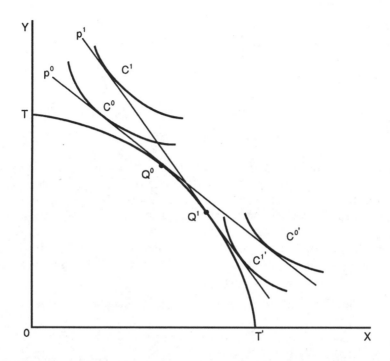

rises, and the larger the share of exports in GNP, the higher the rise in the relative price of the export good X. This is as it should be: the index should go to
1 as trade goes to zero, which D/E does.

Diewert and Morrison multiply the productivity index by the terms-of-trade
index to get a "welfare" index for the combined contributions of productivity
and terms-of-trade change. This "welfare" index is not closely related to the
true utility index but it is certainly easy to compute. The change in real income
or utility is then estimated as:

$$U^1 / U^0 = [A / BC]_*[C]_*[D / E]$$

$$= [\text{productivity}]_*[\text{endowment}]_*[\text{terms-of-trade}] \tag{2.31}$$

The following sections constitute an analysis of changes in technology, factor endowments, and the terms of trade (reflecting a range of foreign changes).
To add concreteness, numerical examples have been used from the GNP function introduced above. This permits the three terms in (2.31) to be computed
using the simulation data to determine if the effects are properly identified by
the Diewert/Morrison approach. The benchmark values for the GNP function
in (2.12) and the Utility function in (2.15) are given in Table 2.1.There is no

Table 2.1

Benchmark Data for Numerical Examples

$p_x = p_y = q_x = q_y = 1$	$L = K = R = 100$	$b = 0.5$

Initial Values of Endogenous Variables

GNP	=	141.42136
U	=	70.71068
X	=	70.71068
Y	=	70.71068
E_x	=	0.0
E_y	=	0.0
w	=	0.70711
r_x	=	0.35355
r_y	=	0.35355

trade initially ($E_x = E_y = 0$), but in some cases the share parameters in the utility function are changed so that there is initial trade. The benchmark equilibrium closely resembles the condition in Figure 2.1, with an equilibrium at A, and an initial world price ratio of pa, so that the economy does not trade, even though trade is possible.

Changes in Endowments

International differences in relative factor endowment have long been recognized as an important source of trade. Indeed, until about a decade ago, these endowment differences formed almost the exclusive focus of international trade theory. In this section, I explore the role of factor endowments, holding technology and world prices constant.

Consider first the effects on the domestic economy of an increase in K, the specific factor used in X (K has been designated as physical capital, but in fact it could be any factor). The effect of the increase in K on the production frontier is shown in Figure 2.3 as a shift from TT' to TT''. An important point for the understanding of production and trade flows is that this shift does not result in anything like a roughly proportional expansion of the two industries. By adding capital to the X sector, we raise the marginal product of labour in that sector. To bring the general-equilibrium system into balance, labour must be drawn from the Y sector, thereby increasing the marginal product of the remaining labour in Y and depressing the marginal product in X. In the new equilibrium, it must be the case that the output of Y has actually fallen. This is

Figure 2.3

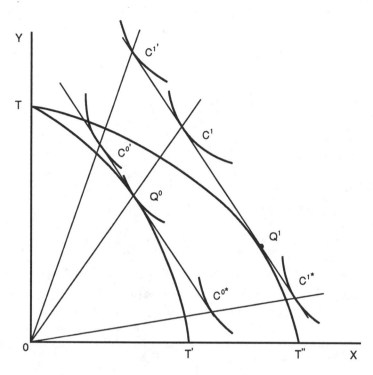

illustrated in Figure 2.3 by the movement of the production point from Q^0 to Q^1. Biased changes over time in a country's factor endowment can lead to strongly biased changes in outputs across industries.

This change in the factor endowment also results in changes in factor prices and therefore in the distribution of income. As was just noted, the increase in K results in a transfer of labour from the Y sector to the X sector. Since the factor ratio (R/L_y) rises in the Y sector, it must follow from (2.6) and (2.7) that the real return to R falls and the real wage rises (commodity prices are constant so real returns are proportional to marginal products).

The change in the real wage can also be seen directly from (2.14). Since w rises, r_x must fall: both factor prices cannot increase in X when p_x is constant. Thus the increase in the endowment of one specific factor reduces the real returns to both specific factors, and increases the return to the mobile factor. These changes have implications not only for the distribution of incomes, but also for longer run factor accumulation and deaccumulation, as noted below.

In order to provide concreteness, consider the technology developed above, and let the endowment of K increase 100 per cent, from 100 to 200. The resulting changes are shown in Table 2.2.

Table 2.2

Change K = 100 to K = 200

Initial Values		New Values	Percent Change
GNP =	141.42136	173.20508	22.47
U =	70.71068	86.60254	22.47
X =	70.71068	115.47005	63.30
Y =	70.71068	57.73502	-18.35
E_x =	0.0	28.86751	inf
E_y =	0.0	-28.86751	-inf
w =	0.70711	0.86603	22.47
r_x =	0.35355	0.28868	-18.35
r_y =	0.35355	0.28868	-18.35

DM index = [prod][endow][tot] = [1.00057][1.22405][1.0]

    = 1.22475

Utility   = 1.22475

L- Prod   = 1.22475

These results illustrate the biased changes in outputs, the income redistribution effect, and changes in trade flows (to be discussed shortly). w changes in verify this, multiply (2.14) through by L.) r_y changes in proportion to Y since specific factors receive constant shares of their sectoral output with Cobb-Douglas technology.

At the bottom of Table 2.2 the Diewert/Morrison (DM) index is shown as three components abbreviated as "prod" (productivity), "endow" (endowments) and "tot" (terms of trade). It can be seen from the example that the index is correct overall and that it identifies the source of the change correctly. There is no productivity change, but a tiny change in [prod] is registered. The index is extremely accurate in this case given the large endowment change. Labour productivity, measured as (GNP)/L is consistent with the other indices.

Now consider the changes in trade flows with reference to Figure 2.3. The model was calibrated in Table 2.1 so there was no trade at the initial equilibrium. Point Q^0 in Figure 2.3 is therefore both the initial consumption and production point. Both goods were given a weight of 0.5 in the Cobb-Douglas utility function (2.15). The endowment change shifts the production point to Q^1 and the consumption point to C^1 in Figure 2.3, thus generating imports of Y and exports of X as shown in Table 2.2. Instead, the share of X in the utility function could have been calibrated at 0.25 rather than 0.5, with the result that initial consumption would be at $C^{0'}$ and final consumption at $C^{1'}$. The endowment change reinforces the direction of trade. If the initial share of X was 0.75, the initial consumption point would be at C^{0*} and the final point at C^{1*} as in Figure 2.3. In this case the effect of the endowment change, in shifting production toward the import-competing sector, reduces the volume of trade. The precise results for this simple model are given in Table 2.3.

Table 2.3

Change K = 100 to K = 200

	EX^0	EY^0	EX^1	EY^1
Share of $C_x = 0.5$	0.0	0.0	28.87	-28.87
Share of $C_x = 0.25$	35.35	-35.36	72.17	-72.17
Share of $C_x = 0.75$	-35.36	35.36	-14.43	14.43

Although a more thorough evaluation appears at the end of this chapter, a few comments regarding the effects of such an endowment change on productivity, trade performance, competitiveness, and real income are warranted at this time.

It is clear that a well specified measure of productivity change should not pick up the change in endowment as a productivity change, and the Diewert/Morrison index does not do so in this case. Real income certainly increases and (as I will emphasize later) productivity increases should not be viewed as somehow "better" than increases in capital stocks.

The example in Table 2.3 reinforces the claim that there should be little intellectual or emotional attachment (at least in the competitive model) to the direction of trade and therefore to trade performance in particular classes of goods. Suppose, for example, that X is a high-tech industry and Y is a resource-based industry, and that R is increased rather than K. Results would then imply a contraction in the production of X with a corresponding decline in exports or an increase in imports of X. However, real income increases to the same extent as if K had been increased in the above example. In the competitive model with constant returns and no distortions, there is no significance to the direction of specialization and trade for real income.

The competitiveness implications of this example are also noteworthy. If the concept were defined in terms of trade performance, then obviously the competitiveness of one industry would tend to rise and the other falls. If, however, competitiveness is defined in terms of productivity or cost, as in the previous chapter, **and** is *ex post* to the labour force adjustment, then competitiveness will not change measured by either productivity or cost definitions. Total factor productivity changes, and although factor prices do change, the change is such that the unit cost of producing the good remains exactly equal to the price. Thus, by a productivity definition, there is no change in competitiveness of either industry, even though the output of Y falls.

One caveat should be added to this interpretation. Y production is unprofitable and uncompetitive at its initial (*ex ante*) level when wage is bid up by the X sector expansion. By shedding labour, the marginal product of labour rises in Y to restore competitiveness at the new wage rate. In this sense, it can be argued that the effect of the increase in K is to reduce the competitiveness of the Y industry.

Finally, consider an increase in L from L = 100 to L = 200. Results are presented below assuming initial budget shares of 0.5 for the two goods in consumption and no trade. Since the production frontier moves out in a radial fashion, there is no trade after the change in L. If the budget share for X was 0.25 or 0.75, then the existing levels of imports and exports would simply increase in proportion to real income.

It should also be noted that the neutral expansion seen here is due to the assumption 1) that the two sectors use labour in the same share and 2) that both sectors have a unity elasticity of substitution between factors. If either assumption were untrue, then there would be no proportional expansion of X and Y and some trade would be generated.

Table 2.4 shows that the accumulation of labour (100 per cent) results in a decline in the real wage, a rise in the returns to both specific factors and, of course, a decline in GNP per worker. Total factor productivity is not affected, but overall labour productivity (GNP/L) drops from 1.41421 to 1.00000 — a drop of 29.29 per cent. To reiterate, total factor productivity is unaffected in this example and competitiveness also remains unchanged — whether defined in terms of trade performance or as per both of the definitions provided in the preceding chapter.

It is interesting at this point to consider briefly the implications of the increase in labour when it is generated by a doubling of efficiency units through training and education, or by a doubling of the labour force participation rate. In the former case, the number of workers remains at 100 and the wage per worker increased from .70711 to 1.00000 (2*.50000). This means that the real wage increases by 41.42 per cent — the same amount as GNP (recall that in the example, labour receives a constant share of GNP). If the labour force participation rate doubles (unlikely, but consider it for the sake of conformity), both the wage per worker and labour productivity decline, as in the Table, but per capita income rises by 41.42 per cent.

Table 2.4

Change L = 100 to L = 200

Initial Values			New Values	Percent Change
GNP	=	141.42136	200.00000	41.42
U	=	70.71068	100.00000	41.42
X	=	70.71068	100.00000	41.42
Y	=	70.71068	100.00000	41.42
E_x	=	0.0	0.0	0.0
E_y	=	0.0	0.0	0.0
w	=	0.70711	0.5	-29.29
r_x	=	0.35355	0.5	41.42
r_y	=	0.35355	0.5	41.42

DM index $= $ [prod] [endow] [tot] $= $ [1.00000] [1.4142] [1.0]
                 $= 1.4142$

Utility $= 1.4142$
L- Prod $= 0.70711$

Changes in Technology

Although there is a substantial body of modern trade theory based on the view that differences in relative factor endowments across countries are the cause of trade, the original writings of Ricardo seem closer to the view that differences in production functions are the cause of trade (Ricardo's theory was primarily normative, so it is difficult to interpret the underlying positive theory).

Suppose that the Hicks-neutral technical efficiency parameter in the X production function is doubled from $q_x = 1$ to $q_x = 2$. The effect on output is then doubled — to twice the amount(s) of the original allocations of both K and L_x — and that output effect is going to be greater than the effect of simply doubling K as analyzed above. The increase in q_x at constant prices increases the marginal products of both K and L_x. With K fixed, general equilibrium is restored by shifting labour from the Y industry to the X industry. The output of Y must fall and the output of X must expand more than a proportional amount to the increase in q_x. The result is essentially the same as that shown in Figure 2.3. Output of Y must fall even though its technology and output price are unchanged.

There is an important difference between factor price changes in response to a change in q_x and changes in response to an increase in K. Since labour is drawn out of the Y industry, (R/L_y) falls; the real return to R must then fall and the real return to L must rise. The difference is the return to K. The level of K is constant and the increase in q_x increases rx proportionately at constant L_x. But in addition, L is drawn into the sector, thus reducing (K/L_x). r_x must increase more than a proportional amount to q_x. These changes are not only of interest from the distributional point of view (which is not the focus of this project), but from the standpoint of long run accumulation and deaccumulation of factors. To preview a later section, the change in q_x can generate an accumulation of K which reinforces the initial output changes. Results using the numerical example developed above are given in Table 2.5.

Table 2.5

Change $q_x = 1$ to $q_x = 2$

Initial Values			New Values	Percent Change
GNP	=	141.42136	223.60680	58.11
U	=	70.71068	111.80339	58.11
X	=	70.71068	178.88544	152.98
Y	=	70.71068	44.72136	-36.75
E_x	=	0.0	67.08204	inf
E_y	=	0.0	-67.08204	-inf
w	=	0.70711	1.11803	58.11
r_x	=	0.35355	0.89443	152.99
r_y	=	0.35355	0.22361	-36.75

DM index = [prod] [endow] [tot] = [1.58114] [1.0] [1.0]
          = 1.58114

Utility   = 1.58114

L- Prod = 1.58114

Again, the strongly biased effects on outputs and factor prices due to the technical change in one sector only can be seen. X sector capital registers the big gain as suggested in the Table. Production of Y declines and imports of Y begin even though Y experiences no change in either total factor productivity or price. Y would, of course, become unprofitable at its original level of production as the price of labour is bid up in line with the discussion in the previous section. By shedding labour, however, the marginal product of labour increases to restore zero profits.

Now consider the effects of a productivity change on trade volumes for different share parameters on X in the utility function as shown in Table 2.3. In the present case, these are given in Table 2.6.

Table 2.6
Change $q_x = 1$ to $q_x = 2$

	EX^0	EY^0	EX^1	EY^1
Share of $C_x = 0.5$	0.0	0.0	67.08	-68.07
Share of $C_x = 0.25$	35.36	-35.36	122.98	-122.98
Share of $C_x = 0.75$	-35.36	35.36	11.18	-11.18

The results here are similar to those in Table 2.3 with one important exception — the technical change in the example is sufficiently strong to reverse the pattern of comparative advantage. This is evidenced by the change in the X share parameter to 0.75 — which ensures that X is initially imported. The biased effect on production is now sufficiently strong to reverse the direction of trade and have X become an export good.

As hinted earlier, the results of the previous section can be used to consider factor-augmenting technical change with just a simple modification. Suppose, for example, that the X production function is given by:

$$X = (q_{xl} L_x)^b (q_{xk} K)^{1-b} \qquad (2.32)$$

The effects of a change from $q_{xk} = 1$ to $q_{xk} = 2$ are shown in Table 2.7.

The effects of a change in q_{xk} from 1 to 2 are the same as those shown in Table 2.2, except that the old value of r_x is now the return to an "efficiency unit" of K. To find the new return per physical unit, simply multiply r_x by q_{xk}. So, in the case of Table 2.7, the return per physical unit of capital is $(2*0.28868) = 0.57736$, an increase of 63.3 per cent over the benchmark. The only other change is that the DM index appropriately shifts the explanation for the change in real income to productivity change. In terms of the notation developed above, C decreases from 1.22405 to 1.0, and the productivity index $[A/(BC)]$ increases from 1.00057 to 1.22475.

Changes in the Terms of Trade

Changes in the terms of trade are an important aspect of this study for several reasons. First, the terms of trade constitute the major mechanism(s) by which changes inside foreign economies are transmitted to our economy. Second, changes in the terms of trade are an important source of real income changes

Table 2.7

Change $q_{xk} = 1$ to $q_{xk} = 2$

Initial Values			New Values	Percent Change
GNP	=	141.42136	173.20508	22.47
U	=	70.71068	86.60025	22.47
X	=	70.71068	115.47005	63.30
Y	=	70.71068	57.73502	-18.35
E_x	=	0.0	28.86751	inf
E_y	=	0.0	-28.86751	-inf
w	=	0.70711	0.86603	22.47
r_x	=	0.35355	0.57736	63.33
r_y	=	0.35355	0.28868	-18.35

DM index = [prod] [endow] [tot] = [1.22475] [1.0] [1.0]

    = 1.22475

Utility = 1.22475

L- Prod = 1.22475

at constant endowments and technology. Third, changes in the terms of trade can generate long run changes in the latter. (These are discussed in the next several sections.) Fourth, it is possible that changes in the terms of trade may be mis-measured as productivity changes. There is some suspicion that the "productivity slowdown" following the 1973 oil-price shock was at least partly due to terms-of-trade changes being identified as productivity changes.

The effect of a change in terms of trade are outlined in Figure 2.2. The price change moves the production point around the production frontier, but that movement has nothing to do with the direction or volume of trade. At exogenous world prices, the effects on production can be analyzed quite independently of consumption and trade. However, Figure 2.2 does show that the effects of a terms-of-trade change on real income have a great deal to do with the direction of trade. If, initially, there is no trade, then *any* change in the terms of trade must make us better off. (This is simply a slight modification of the gains from trade theorem: a country is better off if it can trade at any set of prices other than its autarky prices.) It can be seen, however, that an existing trade volume at the initial price(s) generates an income effect that may reduce real income when the relative price of the imported good rises. The effect of an increase in p_x from 1.0 to 2.0 is shown in Table 2.8.

This Table shows the utility gain for the initially non-trading economy and the redistribution among the various factors — with K the big gainer. There

Table 2.8

Change $p_X = 1$ to $p_X = 2$

Initial Values			New Values	Percent Change
GNP	=	141.42136	223.60680	58.11
U	=	70.71068	79.05694	11.80
X	=	70.71068	89.44272	26.65
Y	=	70.71068	44.72136	-36.75
E_x	=	0.0	33.54102	inf
E_y	=	0.0	-67.08204	-inf
w	=	0.70711	1.11803	58.11
r_x	=	0.35355	0.89443	152.99
r_y	=	0.35355	0.22361	-36.75

DM index = [prod] [endow] [tot] = [1.0076] [1.0] [1.109569]

$\qquad\qquad$ = 1.11800

Utility $\quad$ = 1.11803

L- Prod $\quad$ = 1.58114

are both differences and similarities between this case and the case of a technical shift in q_x analyzed in Table 2.5. The most obvious difference is that between the measure of real income and nominal GNP. This emphasizes the importance of deflating price changes properly, but this problem is well already understood. Note that the same change in real income could have been produced, instead, by cutting p_y to 1/2, but then nominal GNP would have fallen. In any case, the point is that with no trade initially a 100 per cent increase in p_x is inferior to a 100 per cent increase in q_x. In both cases the value of nominal income increases by the same amount, but the consumer's real income increases by less than the nominal increase when p_x is the variable that changes.

The changes in nominal factor prices, and hence the changes in their shares of national income, are exactly the same where p_x and qx are changed, as shown in Table 2.5.

The Diewert/Morrison index is extremely accurate, identifying only a small part of the change in terms of trade as a productivity change, especially when one recognizes how large a change is evaluated. The labour productivity index is simply nominal GNP divided by L, which in itself does not make much sense. If the labour productivity index is divided by the consumer price index, then the result is exactly the same as the change in utility.

Now consider the same price change with the share of X in consumption set first at 0.25 (X initially exported), then at 0.75 (X initially imported).

It can be seen in Table 2.9 that utility increases significantly more than in Table 2.8 since the income effect from the improvement of terms of trade improvement is larger with the larger volume of trade. The Diewert/Morrison index picks up the terms-of-trade effect very accurately. Referring to (2.29), it can be seen that the price change of each good is weighted by the trade shares and thus, for a given price change, the log of the index rises in proportion to the volume of trade. When the utility function was changed, the index was not fooled, however, because the parameter change in utility was translated into trade shares.

Table 2.9

Change $p_x = 1$ to $p_x = 2$, C_x Share in Consumption 0.25

Initial Values			New Values	Percent Change
GNP	=	141.42136	223.60680	58.11
U	=	80.59274	107.15401	32.96
X	=	70.71068	89.44272	26.65
Y	=	70.71068	44.72136	-36.75
E_x	=	35.35534	61.49187	73.93
E_y	=	-35.35534	-122.98373	247.85
w	=	0.70711	1.11803	58.11
r_x	=	0.35355	0.89443	152.99
r_y	=	0.35355	0.22361	-36.75

DM index = [prod] [endow] [tot] = [1.0076] [1.0] [1.31951]
$\qquad$ = 1.32953
Utility $\quad$ = 1.32957
L- Prod $\;$ = 1.58114

Now, consider the results for the share of $C_x = 0.75$.

Table 2.10 shows a case where changes in the terms of trade generate a reduction of real income as well as a change in the direction of trade (I am still unsure how to define the change in the volume of trade when the direction of trade reverses). There is an important lesson in this little example — which is that a correct estimate of a change in real income must take into account any change in the terms of trade. If a change in the terms of trade is ignored and the change in nominal GNP is simply deflated by the index of price change, the result is the Diewert/Morrison term [A/(BC)] [C] — which, in this case, is

Table 2.10

Change $p_x = 1$ to $p_x = 2$, C_x Share in Consumption 0.75

Initial Values			New Values	Percent Change
GNP	=	141.42136	223.60680	58.11
U	=	80.59274	75.76933	-5.98
X	=	70.71068	89.44272	26.65
Y	=	70.71068	44.72136	-36.75
E_x	=	35.35534	5.59017	?
E_y	=	-35.35534	-11.18034	?
w	=	0.70711	1.11803	58.11
r_x	=	0.35355	0.89443	152.99
r_y	=	0.35355	0.22361	-36.75

DM index = [prod] [endow] [tot] = [1.0076] [1.0] [0.92498]

          = 0.93201

Utility   = 0.94015

L- Prod   = 1.58114

equal to 1.0076 and which also suggests that welfare has stayed about the same. Such a finding here would be clearly incorrect; and must be adjusted by applying the terms of trade index.

Note that the alternate procedure used above in deriving the real income function U in (2.19) does this automatically by using the indirect utility function. A change of weights in the utility function is automatically translated into a change in the value of the price index at constant prices. The shift in preferences toward X at $p_x = 2$ in (2.19) increases the magnitude of the price index being used to deflate nominal GNP. The advantage of the Diewert/Morrison approach is that it clearly separates the terms-of-trade effect. Using the real income function (2.19), this effect is buried in the fact that the elasticity of GNP with respect to p_x is greater than the elasticity of the price deflator with respect to p_x if (and only if) the share of X in production is greater than its share in consumption — i.e., if and only if X is exported.

It is reasonable to ask at this point, "How do these results relate to the four central concepts? First, terms-of-trade changes represent a source of large changes in real income that have nothing to do with productivity and factor accumulation. Obviously, there is a change in trade performance, but it must be emphasized that this change is entirely exogenous to the economy. Thus, our search for explanations relating to changes in trade performance must not be confined to domestic causes. Competitiveness certainly changes if its defin-

Figure 2.4

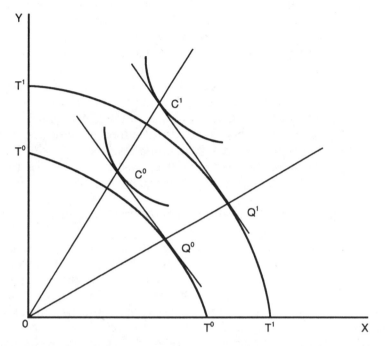

ition is based on trade performance. However, competitiveness does not change at all if its definition is based on a total factor productivity definition. As explained earlier, an increase in p_x reduces profitability and competitiveness in Y at the initial output level (in the *ex ante* sense) as w increases, but competitiveness is restored as labour leaves the industry and the marginal product of remaining labour rises. Following the adjustment, the down-sized Y industry is again competitive.

Some final remarks concerning changes in terms of trade: First, note that an improvement in the terms of trade for the country described in the model can derive from the fact that foreign producers are increasing their productivity in their export (our import) industries. This adjustment is partially passed on to us by lower prices and our real income increases, therefore, even if our import-competing sector in less competitive in the short run. The opposite occurs if foreign producers improve their productivity faster than us in their import-competing (our export) industries. In that case, both our real income and our (short-run) competitiveness in that industry fall. Thus, whether or not we are hurt or helped by an increase in foreign productivity depends entirely upon the sector in which it occurs.

Generally, a uniform increase in foreign productivity helps us. If income elasticities of demand are close to one (preferences are homogeneous), then a uniform outward shift in their production possibilities frontier will lead them to increase both their import demand and export supply at constant prices. This is illustrated in Figure 2.4, where the production frontier of the foreign country shifts from T^0T^0 to T^1T^1 and desired imports and exports increase. If we are not growing and hence not changing our trade offer at constant prices, then the relative price of our exports must increase (or relative price of our imports must fall) to re-establish equilibrium in the market. Our real income rises when there is faster uniform growth in the rest of the world. These findings also underline our government's efforts to lower foreign trade barriers and improve our market access. If successful efforts to reduce foreign trade barriers improve our terms of trade, then the above analysis is applicable. Productivity improvements sound attractive, but increased access to foreign markets can have the same implications for real income.

Capital: Transformation, Accumulation and Trade

I have already suggested that both internal and external changes to an economy can set in motion other processes that reinforce the initial change. This section considers such processes — specifically by making the capital stock endogenous in response to exogenous shocks.

Several different initial exogenous shocks could be considered here: first, a change in R or L, the two exogenous factors; second, an increase in qx; and third, an increase in p_x. In the first "period", the capital stock is constant so there is an impact effect in which only labour can move. In the second period, the capital stock is adjusted. I have chosen to illustrate the problem by changing p_x, but in the second period, the adjustment is exactly the same as if the initial change had been in q_x.

We can consider three alternative senses in which the capital stock can be transformed. Suppose first that R can be transformed into K at an increasing cost. This could be, for example, a group of unskilled workers, who are homogeneous and who are being transformed into skilled workers. All the workers are not equally able to learn, even though all are equal at unskilled work. The first unskilled worker (R) trained is transformed into a very productive skilled worker (K), the second unskilled worker trained is not quite as able as the first and so proves to be somewhat less productive as the skilled worker, etc. A concave transformation function has been chosen such that at the initial values of R and K, R^* units of resources can be transformed into $R^* - (.005)R^{*2}$ units of K.

The situation is first shown in Figure 2.5 where T^0T^0 is the initial production frontier and A is the initial production point at price ratio p^0. An increase in p to p^1 moves production to point B. However, from earlier discussion it is known that the return to K has risen and the return to R has fallen. In the second period, R is transformed into K until the value of the marginal product of the last unit transferred is just equal in the two sectors (note that r_x and r_y will not be equal since the last unit of R transferred yields less than one unit of K: $r_x > r_y$ in long-run equilibrium). The new production frontier T^1T^1 (evaluated given the final supplies of R and K) passes through B and the long-run equilibrium occurs at C, a tangency between T^1T^1 and p^1. The process is reversible: if p^1 falls to p^0, production moves first to B, and then to A as K is transformed back into R.

Table 2.11 shows the numerical results for the movement from B to C in Figure 2.5, where the initial values are those shown as the final values after the price change in Table 2.8. There are several points to recognize in this Table compared to the results shown in Table 2.8.

Table 2.11

$p_x = 2$. **Transform R into K to Reach Long-run Equilibrium**

Initial Values			New Values	Percent Change
GNP	=	223.60680	246.88054	10.41
U	=	79.05694	87.28546	10.41
X	=	89.44272	118.17457	32.12
Y	=	44.72136	10.53141	76.45
E_x	=	33.54102	56.45443	68.31
E_y	=	-67.08204	-112.90886	68.31
w	=	1.11803	1.23440	10.41
r_x	=	0.89443	0.81011	-9.43
r_y	=	0.22361	0.20253	-9.43

DM index = [prod] [endow] [tot] = [1.01496] [1.087808] [1.]
$\qquad$ = 1.10408

Utility $\quad$ = 1.10408

L- Prod $\quad$ = 1.10408

First, the capital transformation reinforces the initial change. The initial increase in px then shifts labour into X, increasing output and increasing the return to K. The second-period effect is to increase the output of X even further. The example, of course, also works in reverse. Reducing the price of X shifts labour out of X, and both the production of X and the return to K decline. The long-run effect is to shift capital to the Y sector, thereby causing a further decline in the production of X. This constitutes the movement from production point B to production point A in Figure 2.5.

Figure 2.5

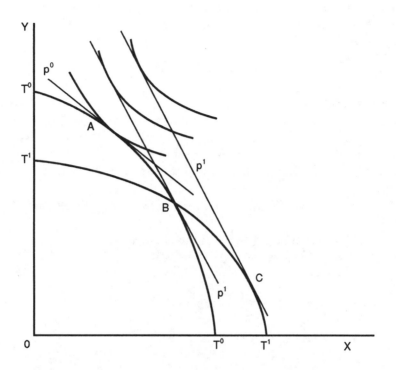

Second, and closely related to the changes in production, the direction of trade is maintained and the volume of trade increases. Thus, responses to changes in terms of trade are more elastic in the long run than in the short run.

Third, the Diewert/Morrison index is correct, although there is a small error in attributing some of the increase to a productivity change (1.5 per cent) and not enough to the endowment effect. It is noteworthy that the endowment is recorded as increasing, even though the total of R and K is falling. This can be explained by the fact that the K that is increasing has a higher value per unit than the R that is decreasing. The net effect of this combination on the C index is seen in equation (2.27).

It is nonetheless true that the index results shown in Tables 2.8 and Table 2.11 are not multiplicative. Suppose the two periods were collapsed into one, and it were possible to compare the initial situation in Table 2.8 to the final situation in Table 2.11. Interestingly, the Diewert/Morrison approach yields the correct overall number, but the decomposition of that number into its component indices is significantly different. The results are presented in Table 2.12 below.

While the overall Diewert/Morrison index is almost exactly correct, it attributes a 10.5 per cent increase to productivity change and shows the factor

---

Table 2.12

Change $p_x = 1$ to $p_x = 2$, and Transform R into K

(Combine the two steps of Tables 2.8 and 2.11)

DM index   =   [prod][endow][tot]

           =   [1.105746] [0.952757] [1.171827]

           =   1.23453

Utility   =   1.23440

---

endowment as falling. Almost half the total change is credited to productivity. The reason for the discrepancy between this result and the combined results of Tables 2.8 and 2.11 is that in this case, the increase in K has a small weight (due to its initially lower price) while the decrease in R has a higher weight (due to its initially higher price). Thus, the factor endowment [endow] listed is shown as falling in value.

It should be clear that Tables 2.8 and 2.11 provide the "correct" combined results, and that Table 2.12 contains misleading results. Productivity, at least in the sense of technical change, has not, in fact, changed.

Now suppose instead that capital can be imported or exported at a fixed price. The rental rate for capital is given by:

$$r_x = (1 - b)p_x q_x L_x^b K^{-b} \tag{2.33}$$

We can solve for L_x using an equation which equalizes the wages in the X and Y sectors. Replace L_x in (2.33) with this value and invert to get the capital demand function.

$$K = [(1-b) q_x(p_x / r_x)]^{1/b}L - [(p_y q_y) / (p_x q_x)]^c R \tag{2.34}$$

The capital demand is homogeneous of degree zero in all prices and homogeneous of degree one in L and R as might be expected. If p_x is changed, what happens to r depends on whether it is fixed in terms of X or Y or some combination thereof. Suppose that r_x is fixed in terms of X so that r_x/p_x is constant — an assumption that will make any change in K in response to a change in p_x smaller than if r_x were fixed in terms of Y. In the latter case, (i.e., r_x fixed in terms of p_y) the first term of (2.34) increases with p_x and the second term falls, while under our assumption (r_x/p_x fixed) only the term (entering with a minus sign) falls.

The situation is shown in Figure 2.6, where A is the initial benchmark equilibrium at price ratio p^0. The increase in the relative price of X to p^1 moves

Figure 2.6

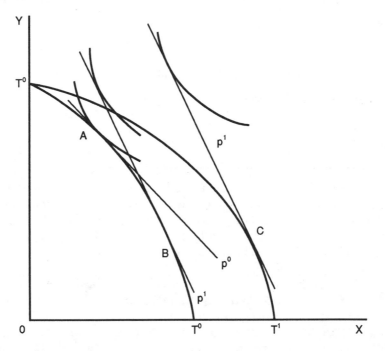

production to point B, as described in Table 2.8 above. But this increases the return to K by more than the increase in p_x, so capital is imported until the marginal product and rental rate are driven down to the old level of r_x/p_x. This generates a movement from B to C as shown in Figure 2.6. The initial increase in X and decrease in Y are reinforced by the movement of capital. Of course, the owners of foreign capital must be paid, but there is still a welfare gain. Foreign owners receive the benefit of the marginal product, but the economy captures "infra-marginal gains" on all but the last unit (i.e., the first unit of capital imported yields the economy the domestic marginal product, but the foreign owner earns only the world rate of return).

Table 2.13 assumes a condition of equilibrium in the initial benchmark data, implying a world price of $r_x/p_x = .35355$. This increases to $r_x/p_x = .44722 = (.89443/2)$ in Table 2.8 when p_x rises. Thus, capital must be imported until r_x/p_x is reduced to the world price of .35355.

Several interesting points are apparent from Table 2.13. First, the ability to borrow from abroad reinforced the initial change, with respect to both production and trade flow. Indeed, the increase in the production of X as capital adjusts (Table 2.13) exceeds its initial increase due to the price change with capital held constant (Table 2.8). Again, this underscores the result that capital

Table 2.13

p_x = 2. Capital is Imported to Reestablish Equilibrium

Initial Values			New Values	Percent Change
GDP	=	223.60680	282.84217	26.49
GNP	=	223.60680	229.80946	2.77
U	=	79.05694	81.25000	2.77
X	=	89.44272	123.74369	38.35
Y	=	44.72136	35.35534	-20.94
E_x	=	33.54102	66.29127	97.64
E_y	=	-67.08204	-79.54941	17.76
w	=	1.11803	1.41421	26.49
r_x	=	0.89443	0.70711	-20.94
r_y	=	0.22361	0.17678	-20.94

Based on GNP

DM index = [prod] [endow] [tot] = [1.02774] [1.] [1.]

$\qquad$ = 1.02774

Utility $\quad$ = 1.02774

Based on GDP

DM index = [prod] [endow] [tot] = [1.00065] [1.264073] [1.]

$\qquad$ = 1.26490

$\qquad$ = 1.02774

mobility generates responses to shocks that are more elastic in the "long run" as capital adjusts. As with the transformation example, this mechanism also works in reverse. A reduction in p_x shifts labour out of X, lowering the return to K by more than the amount of the price reduction, with the result that capital is then lent abroad. The reduced supply of domestic capital further reduces both the production and the export of X. (The reduced supply of domestic capital may also have the effect of increasing imports of X.)

Second, the effect of the borrowing is welfare-improving, but a current account surplus must be run to pay for the capital services. This does not constitute a change in competitiveness in any sense, nor would the converse example (in which capital is exported and a current account deficit is run) signal a loss in competitiveness. The current account balance has no normative significance in this case; it merely implies that it is efficient to trade in factor services as well as to trade in goods.

Third, there are at least two ways to calculate the Diewert/Morrison index. (It is not clear what they are doing about foreign-owned factors.) One method is to use GNP to calculate the A index in (2.25) and use only domestically-owned factors to calculate the C index in (2.27). Following this procedure gives the first number, above, which correctly states the overall value, but attributes it to productivity change (C is 1 since there is no change in domestic endowments). The infra-marginal gains from the investment of foreign capital are therefore attributed to changes in productivity.

A second method is to employ GDP to calculate A and all domestically-used (as opposed to owned) factors to calculate C. This procedure generates the second figure, above, which wildly overstates the gain in real income. (What has, in fact, been estimated is an index that is correct only if the foreign investors had contributed the use of their factors at no cost.) Or, A could be calculated using GNP, and C using total factor supplies, which would generate the productivity index $[A/(BC)] = 0.813038$. According to this calculation, productivity has fallen by 20 per cent.

It follows, therefore, that the existence of foreign-owned factors of production at home when combined with exports of our own factor services abroad may constitute a significant weak link in the relationship between index numbers and real income.

As a final and closely related example, suppose that capital is not traded but is endogenously accumulated and deaccumulated: Assume that domestic consumers discount utility from t periods in the future by the factor $(\exp)(-st)$ where s is the rate of time preference. Assume, too, that consumers maximize the integral of instantaneous utility over an infinite horizon. The steady-state condition is then represented by the (well-known) formula that the rental rate on capital r_x must equal $(s + d)p_k$ where d is the depreciation rate and p_k is the price of a capital good. The present equivalent of (2.33) is then given by:

$$r_x = (s + d)p_k = (1 - b)p_x q_x L_x^b K^{-b} \qquad (2.35)$$

If this equation is inverted and we solve for L_x, as described before equation (2.34), the result is:

$$K = [(s+d)^{-1}(1-b)q_x(p_x/p_k)]^{1/b}L - [(p_y q_y) / (p_x q_x)]^c R \qquad (2.36)$$

Again, let us assume that a unit of capital is produced from one unit of X so that $(p_x/p_k) = 1$ and the first term of (2.36) is a constant. Then, as in the previous case, an increase in p_x from 1 to 2 reduces the (negative) second term so that an additional 75 units of capital will be accumulated over time to restore equilibrium. If the original benchmark data was in equilibrium, then (since $r_x = .35355*p_x$ in that data) (s+d) must equal .35355 in the calibration. Assume that d = .20 and therefore that s = .15355.

The "second period" situation (meaning a comparison of the initial

Table 2.14

p_x = 2. Capital is Accumulated to Reestablish Equilibrium

Initial Values			New Values	Percent Change
GNP	=	223.60680	282.84217	26.49
NNP	=	183.60680	212.84271	15.59
U	=	64.91480	75.25126	15.59
X	=	89.44272	123.74369	38.35
Y	=	44.72136	35.35534	-20.94
E_x	=	23.54102	35.53301	50.94
E_y	=	-47.08204	-71.06602	50.94
w	=	1.11803	1.41421	26.49
r_x	=	0.89443	0.70711	-20.94
r_y	=	0.22361	0.17678	-20.94

Based on GNP

DM index = [prod] [endow] [tot] = [1.000662] [1.264073] [1.]
          = 1.26491

Utility   = 1.159231

Based on NNP

DM index = [prod] [endow] [tot] = [1.001757] [1.157197] [1.]
          = 1.159231

Utility   = 1.159231

response to the price change in Table 2.8 to the new steady state) is as shown in Figure 2.6 assuming net production frontiers are represented with capital stock valued net of depreciation. Table 2.14 records the changes between equilibrium at B and C in Figure 2.6. Note that the initial values of utility and trade are not the same as the initial values in Table 2.13 because depreciation must now be subtracted (some output is used to maintain the capital stock) whereas in Table 2.13 it could be assumed that there was no foreign ownership initially. NNP is net national product; GNP minus depreciation. GNP and GDP are, again, the same.

For the third time, the long-run adjustment effect can be seen reinforcing the short-run effect (Table 2.8). Both the output of X and exports of X increase by more in the long run. The real wage rises significantly in the long run over the short run level. It must be emphasized, however, that a fall in the price of X generates the opposite effect (adjustment). Capital deaccumulates to restore equilibrium, and long-run steady state consumption and instantaneous utility are lower in the steady state than immediately following the price change.

There is nothing suboptimal about this. The increased consumption over the adjustment path, obtained when depreciating capital is not replaced, outweighs the (eventually) lower steady-state of consumption. Consumers are considered to be completely rational and therefore engaged in solving their problem(s) by maximizing full-information along an infinite-time-horizon. Although most researchers and governments track per capita consumption as a welfare indicator, this example does add one caveat to the use of such an indicator.

At the bottom of Table 2.14 a Diewert/Morrison index based on GNP is compared to another index based on NNP. The difference is very large. I have the impression that researchers often track GNP because it is readily available statistically, and they assume that NNP tracks GNP very closely. That would be true here if the endowments of all factors had been increased proportionately. What we have, however, is a very biased change in factor growth as shown in Table 2.14. The problem is that all of the growth is in the one factor that depreciates — so the share of depreciation in GNP is growing. NNP is growing at a considerably slower rate than GNP. Thus, NNP does not track GNP and, moreover, the GNP index greatly overstates real income growth in the steady state.

It must also be added that the NNP index is tricky. The A index is formed by the ratio of NNP in the two "time periods". The weights used in constructing C, however, must include the earnings of capital net of depreciation in the numerators of the share terms, and NNP in the denominator. It can be seen from Table 2.14 that the value of C using NNP is considerably less than the value of C using GNP (gross capital earnings divided by GNP are used for the weights). Using NNP to construct A, but GNP to construct the C index generates the correct overall index, but it also implies that productivity has fallen significantly: $[A/(BC)] = .91705$.

These three examples underscore the cautionary warning that coniderable care should be exercised in constructing and interpreting a link between productivity, endowment, and terms-of-trade indices when capital is endogenous. It is well known that GNP and NNP are not necessarily equivalent and whether or not they track closely is an empirical question. In an open economy with trading in factor services as well as other assets, GNP is not equivalent to GDP. Although GNP is the proper basis for welfare comparison, studies of productivity and trade performance tend to focus on GDP. Such studies therefore tend to provide information about GDP (production), not necessarily about welfare (consumption).

The results of the three experiments described in this section have a number of implications pertinent to the notion of competitiveness, particularly in the long- versus the short-run. In all of the experiments conducted here, the price of the capital-intensive good was increased and a long-run increase in the use of capital was therefore generated. From the standpoint of competitiveness, these price change generated short-run rents for the owners of capital, which would generally be reflected in terms of industry profitability. In the long run, the rents are dissipated as new capital enters the industry, driving down the marginal product of capital. No one makes positive profits over the long run and, indeed, the notion of long-run competitiveness based on profitability has little relevance in the competitive model.

Conversely, a drop in the price of the capital-intensive good lowers the return to capital below its long-run or its international level, and that industry would therefore be seen as unprofitable and/or uncompetitive in the short run. The long-run response is to deaccumulate capital or to ship it abroad, thereby raising the marginal product of the remaining capital to a level of equilibrium. The short-run fall in competitiveness is replaced in the long run by smaller production, smaller exports, and/or higher volumes of imports.

There is therefore a certain link between the notions of competitiveness: the first based on cost and profit considerations; the second based on trade performance. They may not be so completely different, after all — which is why I am suggesting in this section that a positive change in technical efficiency (or terms of trade) may have the effect of increasing cost-competitiveness or profitability in the short run, or increasing trade performance (increased exports or reduced import penetration) in the long run.

Government Policies

Government policies can influence the four key concepts in a number of ways. Such policies can be roughly grouped under two headings: trade policies and domestic policies. While the latter are seldom instituted with trade considerations in mind, in an open economy, they often have significant impact on trade performance and competitiveness. This section focusses primarily on trade policies and their effects — including some major but subtle differences between closely-related policies. Domestic policies are not emphasized in this section because, in the undistorted world of perfect competition, there is little scope for such policies to do much good. I have more to say on this subject, however, in later chapters on industrial organization, externalities and R&D.

A major theme of this section is that, in an open economy two policies may affect production the same way, but the same policies may affect real income in quite different ways. Economists often complain that there is a bias in trade policy and economic journalism toward production instead of consumption. This section reinforces that complaint by presenting examples which, if approached on the basis of focussing on production and associated measures of productivity and competitiveness, are likely to produce results that are completely wrong.

By way of background, the subject of export promotion warrants attention — particularly with respect to the two contrasting ways it is approached by government. First, the government can work to improve access to foreign markets, by having trade barriers (both explicit and implicit) lowered against Canadian goods, by providing marketing assistance, etc. Second, the government can offer direct or indirect subsidies to business interests in the export sector.

Consider the situation shown in Figure 2.7, which initially assumes Canada to be in a state of (unilateral) free-trade equilibrium at production point Q^0 and price ratio p^0. Consumption is at C^0 and X is the export good. Suppose Canada's trading partners have protected markets such that the price received for Canadian exports is less than under global free trade. Assume, in particular, that p^1 is the global free trade price ratio, such that Canada would produce at Q^1 and consume at C^1 under global free trade.

Obviously, the gain to Canada from obtaining free access to foreign markets for Canadian exports carries with it significant welfare benefit, although of course Figure 2.7 does not reflect the administrative costs that might be incurred in the process.

Now, suppose instead that the government turns inward and decides to achieve the same level of X production by subsidizing exports. Also, assume for the moment that Canada is small, such that it faces the fixed world price ratio p^0 in Figure 2.7. The export subsidy raises the domestic price ratio (but not the world price ratio) from p^0 to p^1. Production shifts from Q^0 to Q^1, as before. Trade occurs and finally balances at the world price ratio p^0. The con-

Figure 2.7

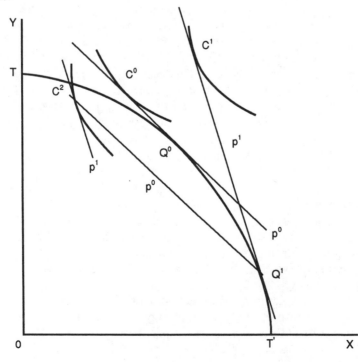

sumption point C^2 is then the point on the world price ratio through Q^1 (which is effectively the country's budget line) where the slope of the indifference curve is equal to the domestic price ratio p^1.

From Figure 2.7 it can be seen that the export subsidy achieves the same change in production as the "improved market access policy", and that the value of production at domestic prices has also changed by the same amount. Although consumers are offered the same prices in the two situations, Figure 2.7 points up a dramatic difference in welfare between the two outcomes. The improved market access increases welfare; the export subsidy reduces welfare. In the case of improved market access, the value of consumption at domestic (and world) prices is the same as the value of production. In the case of the export subsidy, the value of consumption at domestic prices is less than the value of production by the amount of the subsidy. The value of the subsidy payments has a negative income effect that is responsible for the difference between C^1 and C^2 shown in Figure 2.7.

With respect to the expression for real income shown in (2.19) above, tax revenue distributed to, or subsidy costs raised from, consumers must be added or subtracted from "GNP" (the value of production at domestic prices) in order to calculate consumer income at domestic prices. Let NTR denote net tax revenue which is, of course, negative if a subsidy is used. (2.19) should be written as:

$$U = [GNP + NTR](p_x p_y)^{-.5}/2 \qquad (2.37)$$

In the example of improved market access versus export subsidy, GNP and prices are the same in both cases, but under conditions of an export subsidy NTR is negative and real income is reduced.

A numerical example using earlier results is easily constructed. Using Table 2.9, assume an initial world price ratio of $p = 1$, and a share of X in consumption of 0.25. The same initial values are then available as those shown in Table 2.9. The market access policy gives the same values as the "New Values" column in Table 2.9. Table 2.15 compares these values to the values generated by an export subsidy of 100 per cent that generates the same level of X and Y production.

Table 2.15 provides a simple numerical example of the outcomes shown in Figure 2.7. Improved market access and the export subsidy have the same effect on production, but certainly not on consumption and welfare. The export subsidy deteriorates welfare by about 9 per cent from its free-trade level.

Part of the point of this example is that measures of output, such as productivity, that focus entirely on production are likely to miss important effects on real income when these measures are applied to an open economy.

Table 2.15

Comparison of Improved Market Access with an Export Subsidy
World Price of X, $p_x = 1$, Consumption Share of X = 0.25

Initial Values		Market Access	Export Subsidy
GNP	= 141.42136	223.60680	223.60680
U	= 80.59274	107.15401	73.47703
X	= 70.71068	89.44272	89.44272
Cx	= 35.35534	27.95085	19.16629
Ex	= 35.35534	61.49187	70.27643

(U - market access) / (U - free trade) = 1.3296
(U - export subsidy)/(U - free trade) = 0.9117
(U - market access)/(U - export subsidy) = 1.4583

Consider now the matter of trade protection and the effects of an import tariff and a voluntary export restraint. This situation is depicted in Figure 2.8 where the initial free-trade production and consumption points are represented by Q^0 and C^0 at prices p^0. Again, X is the export good. The effect of an import tariff is to raise both the producer price and the consumer price above the world price. Assuming that the economy faces fixed world prices, the import tariff (or, alternatively, an export tax) moves production and consumption to points Q^1 and C^1 respectively as shown in Figure 2.8. The domestic price ratio is p^1, with the tariff increasing the relative price of the import good Y, or decreasing the relative price of the export good X. This result constitutes an unambiguous drop in real income and welfare. The difference between the value of production and the value of consumption at domestic prices (they must balance at world prices) is the value of tariff revenue, as discussed above.

Assume instead that the foreign supplier can be persuaded to limit its exports of Y, with the goal of (our) achieving the same level of production in the good Y (the Canadian industry is import-competing). This is known as the VER, or voluntary export restraint. The foreign country must now restrict its exports of Y sufficiently so that the "world" market clearing price is the same as the distorted domestic price ratio p^1 under the tariff. At the appropriate level of the export restraint (when targeted on domestic production the level of exports is not necessarily the same as the level under the tariff), Q^1 is again the domestic production point. However, p^1 is now the world price as well as the domestic price ratio, and so the country must trade at p^1 not p^0.

Figure 2.8

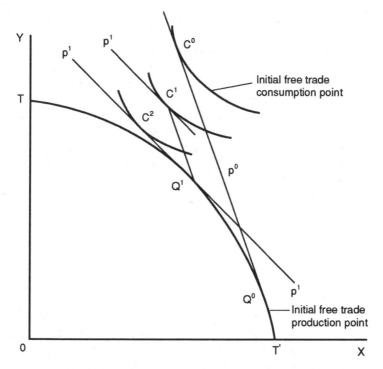

The consumption point achieved under the VER is point C^2 in Figure 2.8. This point is welfare inferior to C^1 and it can be demonstrated that the difference in real income between the two points is exactly equal to the revenue collected under the tariff but which implicitly accrues to the foreign supplier under the VER. Here again, is an example of two policies that have exactly the same effect on production and production-based measures of income, etc., but the effects on real income are quite different.

A numerical example can be constructed using the results of Table 2.9 for most of the data. Assume that the initial price ratio is now $p_x = 2$, and that a 100 per cent tariff lowers the domestic price ratio to $p_x = 1$. The "New Values" in Table 2.9 now become the Initial Values of Table 2.16 and vice versa.

It can be seen from the results shown in Table 2.16 that a VER is a significantly inferior way to achieve a production target than an import tariff, because of the consumption loss from the lost tariff revenue under the VER. In our example, the country exercising the VER achieves a 58 per cent increase in the production of Y over the free trade level at the cost to the importing country of a 25 per cent loss of real income. In addition, it can be shown that a tariff is inferior to a production subsidy, since a tariff distorts consumption as

Table 2.16

Comparison of an Import Tariff with a Voluntary Export Restraint
World Price of X, $p_x = 2$, Consumption Share of X = 0.25
VER Chosen to Yield Same Domestic Production as Tariff

Voluntary Restraint		Tariff	Free Trade
GNP	= 141.42136	141.42136	223.60680
U	= 80.59274	96.71130	107.15401
X	= 70.71068	70.71068	89.44272
Y	= 70.71068	70.71068	44.72136
C_x	= 35.35534	42.42641	27.95085
C_y	= 106.06602	127.27922	167.70509
E_x	= 35.35534	28.28427	61.49187
E_y	= -35.35534	-56.56854	-122.98373
	(U - tariff) / (U - free trade) = 0.9025		
	(U - VER) / (U - free trade) = 0.7521		
	(U - VER) / (U - tariff) = 0.8333		

well as production, whereas a production subsidy distorts only production. Once again, this underlines the fact that trade policy can — and does — have effects that are not captured by production-side measures.

The implication of these results for measures of competitiveness are much the same as those discussed in the previous section (in connection with changes in the terms of trade). The short-run effect of changes in trade policy is to generate short-run rents for specific factors (i.e., equity owners) in favoured sectors, and/or short-run losses for specific factors in disadvantaged sectors. Trade policy changes thus trigger changes in short-run competitiveness based on a cost or profitability definition. In the longer run, these changing cost/profit conditions generate a movement (or an accumulation/deaccumulation) of factors, which are ultimately manifested as changes in the output and trade levels of an industry. The trade performance and cost-based definition of competitiveness are not at odds with each other. Rather, one applies in the short run, the other in the longer run.

One qualification of this argument should be noted. If costs are compared across countries, then a subsidized export industry or a protected import industry will have higher prices — and hence higher costs — than its foreign competitors. This is due to the effect of trade policy driving up the prices of the specific factors upon which those industries are dependent. Although this observation of non-competitiveness is valid, it should not be construed as evidence that an industry cannot exist in the absence of a policy. The removal of a policy causes an industry to downsize until the returns to the specific factors in that industry are sufficiently reduced to make the industry competitive at world prices. A more accurate description of the effects of protection/subsidies is that they imply that an industry is uncompetitive at current levels of production.

Although more will be said about policies that affect factor markets in later chapters, there is one point related to factor market distortions that should be dealt with here. Factor market distortions generally have the same effects as those presented in Figures 2.7 and 2.8, but they also have the additional effect of causing production to take place interior to the efficient production frontier. This cannot happen in the specific-factors model used here because, with only one factor mobile between sectors, production always takes place on the efficient production frontier unless the nature of the distortion is such that some factors are unemployed (e.g., as with a minimum wage distortion). It does not seem to be worthwhile to develop an additional analysis here since few new points would appear. It is possible, however, that some factor market distortions (or their removal) could show up in productivity measures. For example, in a productivity study using a highly aggregated measure of capital, a distortion that causes capital to be allocated inefficiently across sectors could show up as a measured decrease in productivity rather than as a reduction in the value of the capital stock.

Summary and Empirical Evaluation

There have been many studies on the competitive, general equilibrium model, but the majority have been focussed on testing the factor-proportions theory of trade, i.e., testing whether or not international differences in factor endowments are the major explanation of trade. Some work has tested this theory against the alternative hypothesis that there are differences in production technologies across countries and/or scale economies in production.

Empirical support for the factor-proportions theory has been weak — at least relative to the tremendous amount of space economists have devoted to the theory in their research and writings. Authors such as Leamer (1984) and Maskus (1985) found some support for the theory. But later works by Bowen, Leamer, and Sveikauskas (1987), Dollar, Wolff, and Baumol (1988), and Brecher and Choudhri (1988) reported very weak evidence. Studies by Bowen et al. and Dollar et al. found evidence that production technologies are not the same across countries. The latter also found evidence of scale economies in 16 out of 28 industries. However, when a model with both scale economies and differences in technology is tested, the scale economies lose significance.

The evidence thus suggests that there is only weak support for the notion that differences in factor endowments are the principal cause of trade. There is support for the view that technologies are different across countries. The

Dollar et al. result on scale economies is not convincing because what they are calling scale economies is productivity related to the level of employment in an industry (national level scale economies) and not scale economies at the level of the firm. This type of scale economy thus postulates that efficiency is related to country size. However, in a world in which the major industrialized countries are closely integrated, there is no good justification for this type of scale economies. This is an important issue for trade policy and is considered in more detail later in this study.

The validity and relevance of this chapter to the four concepts does not depend upon whether trade is caused by differences in factor endowments or by differences in technologies. (Note that very little has been said in this chapter about precisely how the country in question differs from its trading partners.) None of the general findings in this chapter depend on the endowments versus technology model of trade. Indeed, the findings are also valid for trade caused by other international differences such as differences in preferences.

The key assumptions upon which the analysis of this chapter rests are: constant returns to scale, and perfect competition. With perfect competition (and no distortions), markets tend to allocate resources efficiently, and thus the concept of trade performance changes has no direct relevance to real income measures. Indeed, almost everything the government does (except when it has monopoly power in trade) is welfare-reducing. The direction and volume of trade, as well as the level of industry outputs have no normative significance. Competitiveness, as has been noted several times, is a positive description of the conditions in an industry; it is not necessarily a normative description. Any change in the domestic or foreign economy generates short-run changes in which some industries become more competitive and others become less competitive in terms of cost and profits. In the long run, these translate into changes in industry size and the volume of trade which are an alternative definition of competitiveness. Rents or losses in the short run, size and trade performance changes in the long run. But whether any particular change is "good" or "bad" depends upon the circumstances. A price change is "good" if it represents an improvement in the terms of trade; it is "bad" if it constitutes a deterioration of the terms of trade. Thus, a price change can be evaluated only if the direction of trade is known. World price increases for imports that improve the "competitiveness" of our import-competing industries cannot improve real income in the competitive model. Related comments were made concerning the macro interpretation of competitiveness based on the current account balance.

There is considerable evidence that for many industries, scale economies and imperfect competition do exist. Externalities and spillovers in R&D have been identified. Under these assumptions, the levels of firm and in some cases industry outputs do have normative implications. Changes in trade barriers and in the terms of trade, which have essentially zero effects on properly constructed productivity measures in the competitive model, may have significant productivity implications when imperfect competition, scale economies, and externalities are present. Measures of competitiveness based on trade performance, which have no normative content in the competitive model, may have implications for real income. Some policies which are simply merchantilist and welfare-reducing in the competitive model can also be welfare-improving. These topics are considered in the next chapter.

Where, then, do we stand and how do we evaluate the competitive model? My personal view is an eclectic one. I believe that multiple causes of trade exist simultaneously, and that some industries can be safely categorized as perfectly competitive while others are obviously oligopolistic. I believe that differences in factor endowments and differences in production technologies are very important causes of trade. I support that notion that there is much competition, and that actual trade patterns are "good" indicators of comparative advantage. The results of this chapter are then a good basic guide. But the results must be strongly qualified in industries that have strong scale economies, both internal and external.

There has been much written lately on productivity and technology, and there may be some belief that these might be superior avenues to increasing real income relative to other alternatives. This chapter identifies three other options to increasing real income in addition to increasing total factor productivity. These are: 1) increases in factor endowments, particularly with respect to capital stocks, 2) improvements in international terms of trade, and (3) more effective trade policy. All of these are important potential sources of economic growth, and it is not at all clear whether a dollar invested in any one of these areas might not be more productive than a dollar invested in R&D.

Bear in mind that productivity is a residual. Suppose that investment in R&D creates intangible knowledge capital while investment in plant and equipment increases measured capital stocks. The former increases measured "productivity"; the latter does not. Shifts between the accumulation of knowledge capital and the accumulation of physical capital affect measured productivity, but may have little effect on the growth of real income. The point is that care must be taken not to "overload" the notion of productivity with too much normative significance relative to other sources of economic growth. The fact is that at this time we do not know whether or not a dollar invested in R&D yields more benefit than a dollar invested in new plant and equipment or in education and training.

The Industrial-Organization Model

Introduction

Although there has always been a tradition of industrial organization at the applied level in Canada, formal trade theorists, until about 1980, concentrated almost exclusively on the competitive, constant-returns model. Melvin, in his *Canadian Journal* article in 1969 was, perhaps, the first to demonstrate — by means of a very simple general-equilibrium model — that scale economies offer potential gains from trade even for two absolutely identical economies. Studies by Eastman and Stykolt (1967) and Paul and Wonnacott (1967) also made important contributions by arguing the importance of industrial-organization effects in a small open economy.

Since the mid-1960s, much has been written analyzing various industrial organization dimensions of Canadian industry, particularly with respect to the manufacturing sector. Some of the best works in recent years are the counter-factual computable-general-equilibrium analyses by Richard Harris (1984), and Harris and Cox (1984), and the factual econometric and data studies of Baldwin and Gorecki (1983a, b, c, d, 1985, 1990). These and other studies demonstrate the quantitative importance of industrial-organization effects. They also reinforce the claim that industrial-organization effects are not simply minor curiosities (marginally ruffling the conclusions of the competitive model), but that they are significant in themselves.

This chapter explores the implications of the industrial-organization approach for the four central concepts. As in the previous chapter, a simple general-equilibrium model has been developed that is used repeatedly to analyze variations of the basic model. The model has only one factor — labour — but technical efficiency or labour productivity can differ across countries, so the model can also have a Ricardian (comparative advantage) dimension. However, the importance of non-comparative advantage trade (trade not based on differences between countries) will be clear.

The fundamental modification to the competitive model adopted here is the introduction of scale economies or decreasing average cost in some industries. Generally, competitive market structures generally cannot be supported by such technologies so, theoretically and empirically, scale economies are associated with imperfect competition. It is important to note that imperfectly competitive market structures result from scale economies, not the other way around. Government policy cannot simply banish imperfect competition without precipitating shut downs of the industries in question. Conversely, in a free market economy, imperfect competition cannot exist in the long run without scale economies due to entry of new firms. (Of course, departures from free markets, such as regulation and licensing, can allow long-run monopoly rents to exist).

Several variables that have no positive or normative significance in the competitive model (especially firm scale) now become important. Firm scale (output per firm) affects both measures of productivity and real income, although neither relationship occurs in the competitive model. Because of this, changes in firm scale imply quite different roles for and effects of public policies. Under certain conditions, policies that are simply merchantilist in the competitive model become welfare-improving in the industrial-organization models.

A Simple Model with Fixed Costs

Suppose there are two goods (X and Y) produced in an economy from a single factor, labour (L), which is in fixed supply ($L = L_x + L_y$). Assume further that Y is produced with constant returns to scale by a competitive industry so that units can be chosen such that $Y = L_y$. If Y is chosen as numeraire ($p_y = 1$), the wage rate in terms of Y will also equal 1 and p will denote the price of X in terms of Y, with the cost of producing X given simply by L_x. Assume that the production of X has an initial fixed cost, given as F, and a constant marginal cost, m. The total cost of labour required to produce X is then $L_x = F + mX$. This is the real cost function for X.

The production frontier for this economy is shown in Figure 3.1 as TFT'. $T = L$ is the maximum output of Y when $X = 0$. To begin producing X, the fixed cost TF must be invested before any output is realized. Thereafter, the constant marginal cost of producing X is shown by the liner segment FT' which has a slope equal to m.

The average cost of producing X is simply total cost (L_x) divided by output, or:

$$AC_x = L_x / X = (L - L_y) / X = (T - Y) / X \qquad (3.1)$$

where T is the maximum possible output of Y. (See Figure 3.1). Consider points A, B, and C in Figure 3.1. Equation (3.1) shows, for example, that the average cost of producing X at A is simply the slope of the line passing through T and A. This is similarly the case for B and C. From Figure 3.1 it can also be seen that the average cost of X falls with increases in the output of X or, alternatively, that production of X is characterized by increasing returns to scale. The average cost of producing X is:

$$AC_x = L_x / X = m + F/X \quad \text{implying } X / L_x = [AC]^{-1} \tag{3.2}$$

Note that labour productivity and total-factor productivity (since labour is the only factor) now vary directly with output, unlike the situation in the competitive constant-returns model. If an empirical analysis imposes constant returns on the technology, any change in the output of the X industry will be reflected as a change in "productivity". An increase in output, therefore, is an increase in productivity.

An important point for purposes of this discussion is that the equilibrium price ratio must cut the production frontier if positive X is produced. If production occurs at point B, for example, the price ratio p must be no less (flatter) than the average cost of X given by the slope of TB. The slope of the production frontier represents marginal cost, which is less than average cost with increasing returns to scale.

Figure 3.1

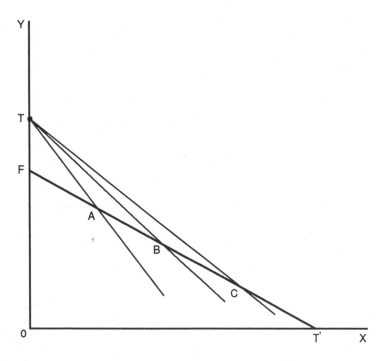

An equilibrium with strictly positive profits for a monopoly producer of X is shown in Figure 3.2 where the price ratio p^m through the equilibrium point A is steeper than the average cost of X represented, again, by the slope of TA. Point G represents the GNP in terms of Y; GNP (0G where 0 is the origin) is composed of wage income in terms of Y (0T) and profits in terms of Y (TG). The budget line of wage earners is shown as a line with slope p^m through Y = T. Since wage earners' income is fixed in terms of Y at Y = T, a decrease in p always increases wage earners' utility or real income (their budget line rotates around the fixed point T). Wage income equals GNP if profits are zero.

Figure 3.2

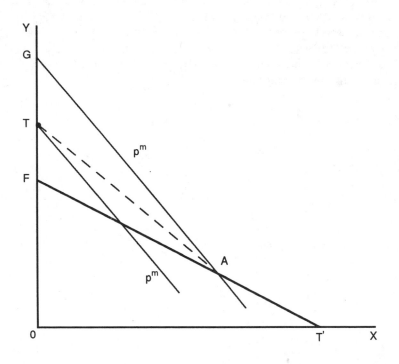

Sources of Real Income and Productivity Gains from Trade

There are five conceptually separate sources of gains from trade in the presence of scale economies and imperfect competition:
- Decreasing Average Cost
- Pro-Competitive Gains
- Exit of Redundant Firms
- Increased Product Diversity
- Specialized Plants and Inputs

DECREASING AVERAGE COST

Suppose a monopoly producer of X in the home country prices X at average cost (as in a regulated monopoly or as in a contestable-markets model). Initial equilibrium is shown at point A in Figure 3.3 at price ratio p^a. Now suppose that a second identical country is introduced as a competitor and that only one producer survives in the trade as a consequence to having to lower its prices to the level of average costs (again, as in the contestable-markets model). Assume arbitrarily that the home-country firm survives, (an assumption that really makes no difference in this case).

Figure 3.3

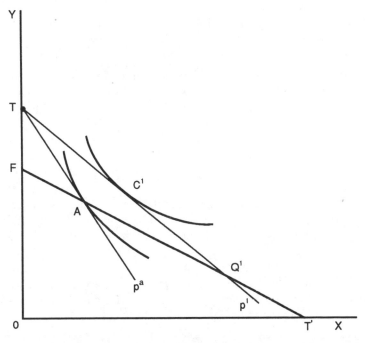

One possible outcome is that the home firm will double output (MC is constant) given double the market size, producing at point Q^1 (in Figure 3.3) with a lower price and average cost represented by p^1. Half the output is exported to the foreign country to achieve a consumption point at C^1. The identical foreign country enjoys the same consumption bundle, but produces at point T.

Both countries gain due to the lower price of X. The home country gains as a result of increased production at lower average cost, while the identical foreign country gains by replacing costly domestic production with a lower cost import. The home country registers an increase in labour productivity in the X industry. Real wages in both countries are unchanged in terms of Y and are increased in terms of X.

Note in this example that it is of no significance which country specializes in X and which specializes in Y. Both countries enjoy, equally, the benefits of concentrating production of the increasing-returns good in one country. This is not always the case, however. (Anticipating results in the next section), problems can arise in a country when its firm stays in business but reduces production, effectively moving from an initial point Q^1 to a point such as A (see Figure 3.3). The general message for assuring welfare gains is "be big or begone". The sin is not in exiting an industry; it is in producing too many goods at too small a scale.

PRO-COMPETITIVE GAINS

Refer now to Figure 3.4 and assume that a monopolist makes positive profits in autarky. Autarky equilibrium is given at point A at price p^0. Pure pro-competitive gains can now be illustrated by the numerical example shown in the section on Possible Losses from Trade, although it is, admittedly, a somewhat fanciful case. Suppose a second country with a monopoly producer is added, and that the two producers identified in the case just discussed play a Cournot game when trade occurs (each producer behaves as if the other producer's output is fixed). Under trading conditions, the firms now perceive their demand curves as more elastic and so increase their outputs (other things equal). If the parameters are now juggled a little (so as to reduce the size of the foreign country or to lower marginal cost as discussed in the section on Possible Losses from Trade), a solution can be engineered in which the home firm continues to produce its autarky output, but at a lower price. Figure 3.4 shows this very special case where the price has been driven down to p^*, the average cost of producing at A. Although the average cost has not changed, consumers move from A to C and thus gain from trade. The increase in consumers' surplus attributable to the pro-competitive price reduction outweighs the loss of monopoly profits to the domestic firm. There is also a redistribution of income away from profits to factor owners.

Figure 3.4

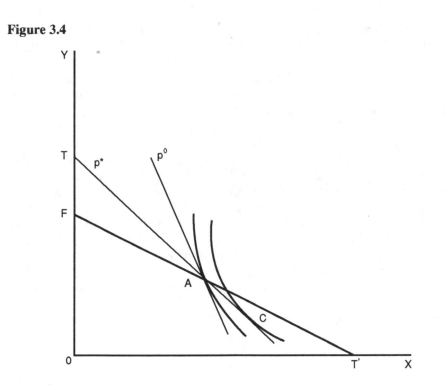

In the example shown in Figure 3.4, there is no measured gain in productivity, although the Diewert/Morrison index (as discussed in the previous chapter) would register an improvement in the terms-of-trade (the good with the increased price has positive exports *ex post*).

EXIT OF REDUNDANT FIRMS
Scale economies pose something of a dilemma with respect to the number of firms in an industry. On the one hand, a small number of firms is desirable from the standpoint of technical efficiency. If the average-cost curve for a firm is everywhere downward sloping (as in the current example), it is desirable to have the entire output of the industry produced by a single firm. On the other hand, a small number of firms generally registers a larger market power distortion as well as a smaller total output. This tradeoff for a single economy gives rise to a third source of gains from trade. Combining two identical countries, it is possible to have more firms competing in total and, at the same time, fewer firms in each country, individually. For example, each country could have five firms in autarky and four firms supported in free trade, with eight then competing in total in free trade. Such an outcome tends to occur in a model with Cournot competition and free entry. (This, too, is discussed in the section on Possible Losses from Trade.)

This situation is illustrated in Figure 3.5 where A is the point of autarky equilibrium for each of two identical countries. Free entry has forced the price down to the level of average cost and the vertical distance TF is now interpreted as the combined fixed costs of the existing firms. Trade causes each Cournot firm to perceive its demand curve to be more elastic, causing each to increase output. However, this leads to negative profits (losses) and the exit of some firms. Equilibrium is restored at a lower price p^* with fewer firms in each country individually, but more firms in total. The elimination of the redundant firms frees up the resources that were devoted to fixed costs and the production frontier of each country shifts to TFT''. Trade will depend on where an indifference curve tangent to p^* is positioned. Consumption has been arbitrarily drawn at exactly point Q^*, the new production point: there is no net trade.

There are several observations to be made from Figure 3.5. First, the number of firms in the open economy has, at best, an ambiguous relationship to competitiveness and real income. The diagram clearly points out that measures of competition should not necessarily be drawn only from the number of domestic firms. Second, the elimination of some firms does not necessarily signal a decrease in total domestic production of the good. Third, factor productivity and real income increase in this example (as they do in the case

Figure 3.5

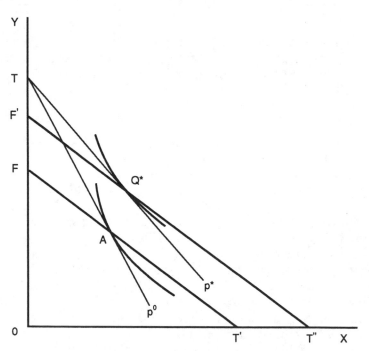

represented by Figure 3.3) — for reasons that have nothing to do with either technical change or trade performance. Note that the indifference curve could as easily have been drawn tangent to p^* below Q^* in Figure 3.5 with the trade result that X is imported. Productivity, real income, and competitiveness (in the sense of efficiency) are linked to firm scale, not to industry scale or to the direction of trade.

INCREASED PRODUCT DIVERSITY

Gains from trade in the form of increased product diversity have been emphasized in a series of studies undertaken by Krugman (1979), Lancaster (1980), Helpman (1981), and Ethier (1982). This situation is shown in Figure 3.6, which assumes that both X and Y are produced with IRS. Production functions for goods X and Y are identical, and the goods are symmetric but imperfect substitutes in consumption. Due to large fixed costs, it is in a country's interest in autarky to produce only one good. A country can produce both goods, but producing only one good at either point T or point T is more efficient. Again, if two identical countries are considered together, each can specialize in one of the goods, trade half the output of its good for half the output of the other

Figure 3.6

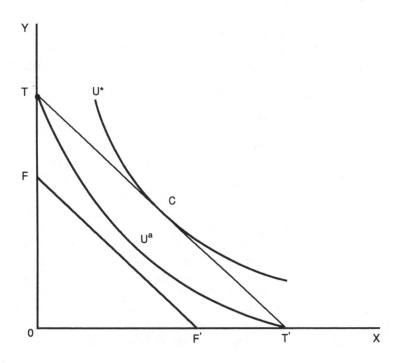

country's good, and both will capture a gain from trade. Each country can reach point C as shown in Figure 3.6.

In the situation shown in Figure 3.6, there is no increase in firm scale or in factor productivity as a consequence of trade. Measures of productivity and real output will register no change, nor will changes in scale economies be detected. Yet there are certainly scale economies and a gain in real income. The scale economies show up by limiting the number of goods produced in autarky. The gains from trade are in the form of more goods available at the same costs as the old, rather than in the form of the same goods at lower costs, as shown in Figures 3.3, 3.4 and 3.5.

The problem posed by the appearance of "new goods" and their possible effect on index numbers for real income has been recognized, but little has been done about this (Feenstra and Markusen, 1990 is, perhaps, the exception). The difficulty is that utility is measured by income and is not directly observable. So, if a consumer gets one apple and one orange instead of two apples for the same total price, utility goes up due to increased diversity, but the index of real consumption of fruit is listed as unchanged. There is some suspicion among researchers that the lack of any provision for new goods in the index numbers may constitute asignificant source of error — underestimation — related to the growth of real income over the last several decades. No quantitative evidence is yet available, however.

SPECIALIZED PLANTS AND INPUTS

Increases in market size due to trade may also enable firms to build more specialized plants with fewer product lines and also to create specialized inputs. The first of these two effects has been well documented by Baldwin and Gorecki. (I am not aware of any empirical work that addresses the creation of specialized intermediate inputs, but theoretical works have been published by Ethier, 1982, and Markusen, 1989 and 1990b.) Figure 3.6 can be used with indifference curves now interpreted as isoquants for final output. The creation of specialized inputs (increases in the division of labour) requires an initial fixed cost TF or $\overline{T}\,\overline{F}$. Two countries in autarky each create only one such input — as shown by the simple example in Figure 3.6 (e. g., general purpose machinery). Output level U^a is achieved in each country from the amount of resources devoted to the production of this particular good by each country. Combining the countries through trade, the creation of two specialized inputs (dedicated machinery) is profitable and the output level U^* can be attained from the resources that previously produced only U^a.

Unlike the case of differentiated final goods, the gains from the creation of specialized intermediate inputs can be picked up by productivity measures, since output is measured in terms of actual output. There is a danger, however, that the source of the productivity increase may be incorrectly attributed to technical changes, rather than to trade liberalization or to growth in the rest of the world. As already stated, productivity is measured (as opposed to defined) as an unexplained residual that lumps together a number of different causal factors.

Producer services, such as those of management and engineering consultants, are specialized intermediate inputs created with large learning costs (see Markusen, 1989). It is important to have access to these services from abroad if Canadian industry is to be competitive.

Possible Losses from Trade and the Gains-from-Trade Theorem

The gains-from-trade theorem can be expressed simply using the revealed-preference criterion. According to the revealed-preference criterion: a sufficient condition for gains from trade is that the value of free-trade consumption at free-trade prices exceeds the value of autarky consumption at free-trade prices. Let superscript f denote quantities in a free-trade equilibrium, and let superscript a denote the autarky equilibrium. Then:

$$p^f C_x^f + C_y^f \geq p^f C_x^a + C_y^a \tag{3.3}$$

The balance-of-payments condition in the free trade and the autarky market-clearing conditions are:

$$p^f C_x^f + C_y^f = p^f X^f + Y^f, \quad C_x^a = X^a, \quad C_y^a = Y^a. \tag{3.4}$$

Substituting (3.4) into (3.3), the sufficient condition for gains from trade is:

$$p^f X^f + Y^f \geq p^f X^a + Y^a \tag{3.5}$$

The total labour endowment L is divided between the two sectors according to:

$$L = (AC_x^i)X^i + Y^i, \qquad i = f, a \tag{3.6}$$

Subtract (3.6) from the left side of (3.5) (i = f) and from the right side (i = a). (3.5) then becomes:

$$(p^f X^f - (AC_x^f)X^f) + (Y^f - Y^f) \geq$$
$$(p^f X^a - (AC_x^a)X^a) + (Y^a - Y^a) \tag{3.7}$$

which simplifies to:

$$(p^f - AC_x^f)X^f \geq (p^f - AC_x^a)X^a \tag{3.8}$$

Substituting in the equation for AC_x in (3.2), this reduces (the terms in F cancel) to the simple condition:

$$(p - m)X^f \geq (p - m) X^a \text{ or, since } p > m, \ X^f \geq X^a. \tag{3.9}$$

Expansion in the output of the increasing returns sector is a sufficient condition for gains from trade. The intuition is that, with the price of good X in excess of marginal cost, there is an added welfare effect $(p_x - m)dX$ from any change in the output of X, dX. p_x is the value of an additional unit to consumers while m is the cost of producing an additional unit. This additional welfare effect, which is positive only if output expands, must be tacked onto the usual gains-from-trade effect.

Figure 3.7 shows what can go wrong. Initial equilibrium is at A, with price ratio p^*. Free trade production is at Q^1, consumption at C^1, with the price ratio p^1. The welfare loss due to the contractionary effect of X production outweighs other sources of gains from trade and welfare is reduced. It is unclear as to how likely this might be, although a case based on these parameters is constructed in the following section. It is virtually impossible to construct such a case with free entry and exit.

Note that the production expansion condition is sufficient — but not necessary — for gains from trade. Figure 3.7 could have been constructed with the

Figure 3.7

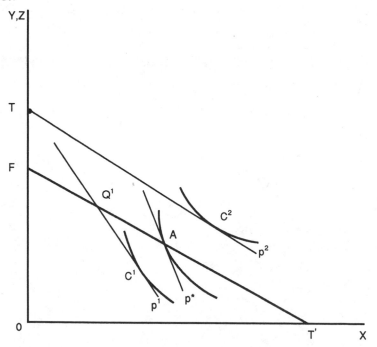

price ratio p^1 sufficiently flat that it cuts through the indifference curve through point A, thus giving a superior consumption level. Or, consider the case where the world price is sufficiently low to drive the country out of X production and into specialization in Y. This is illustrated in Figure 3.7 with A again denoting the autarky equilibrium and C^2 denoting the free-trade consumption point at price ratio p^2.

As previously noted, the country gets into difficulty as a small producer of the IRS good. There is a general implication in favour of either being a big producer or getting out of the industry. However, a small country cannot be a large producer in all industries. A policy of industrial diversity, as advocated by some in Canada, is a potential disaster. Productivity, competitiveness and real income all suffer. Conversely, countries such as Sweden, Denmark, and Switzerland have done very well indeed by adopting policies of industrial specialization.

A Model of a Cournot Duopoly

This section provides a concrete example of the possible gains and losses discussed above. Suppose the home country has a single producer of good X, and the foreign country has a single producer of good Y, which may or may not be a perfect substitute for X. Z will denote the competitive, constant-returns good which can be produced in both countries. The utility function for consumers in both countries is given by a quadratic equation (3.10), where C_i is now interpreted as consumption per person.

$$U = aC_x - (b/2)\, C_x^2 + aC_y - (b/2)\, C_y^2 - cC_xC_y + C_z \qquad (3.10)$$

Z is produced from one unit of the single factor L, as before, so the aggregate budget constraint for consumers is:

$$L + PR_x = (C_z + p_xC_x + p_yC_y)L \qquad (3.11)$$

where PR_x denotes the profits of the X producer, assumed to enter the domestic income stream. Maximization of (3.10) subject to (3.11) gives simple linear inverse demand functions.

$$p_x = a - bC_x - cC_y, \quad p_y = a - bC_y - cC_x \quad c \leq b. \qquad (3.12)$$

There is a zero income-elasticity of demand for X and Y (all additional income at constant prices is spent on Z). $c = b$ in (3.12), indicates that X and Y are perfect substitutes, while $c < b$ indicates that X and Y are imperfect substitutes. In the closed (autarky) economy, C_x equals (X/L). Y is not available. For simplicity, set $L = 1$. Profits for the X producer, expressed as PR_x, are given by p_xX minus variable costs m_xX and minus fixed costs, F.

$$PR_x = (a - b (X/L)) X - mX - F = (a - bX) X - mX - F \qquad (3.13)$$

Maximizing this function gives the autarky monopoly output of X.

$$X^a = (a - m_x) / (2b) \quad \text{at } L = 1. \qquad (3.14)$$

Now assume a free-trade equilibrium in which there are no tariffs or transport costs between the home and the foreign country. Per person consumption of X and Y are now total world production divided by total world population. Let total world population be given by D. D = 2 indicates that the two countries are of the same size (it has already been assumed that L = 1). Values of D greater than one indicate that the home country is the smaller of the two.

The profit equations for the producers of good X and good Y are:

$$PR_x = (a - b (X/D) - c(Y/D)) X - m_x X - F \qquad (3.15)$$

$$PR_y = (a - b (Y/D) - c(X/D)) Y - m_y Y - F \qquad (3.16)$$

The Cournot assumption is that each producer regards the output of the other producer as constant. The first-order conditions for (3.15) and (3.16) can be solved to yield two equations which are generally referred to as Cournot reaction functions.

$$X = (a - m_x) / (2b/D) - (c/(2b)) Y \qquad (3.17)$$

$$Y = (a - m_y) / (2b/D) - (c/(2b)) X \qquad (3.18)$$

Both these equations in two unknowns can be solved to show the Cournot equilibrium level of X production in free trade.

$$X^f = \{2(a - m_x) / (2b)\} [D2b^2 / (4b^2 - c^2)]$$

$$-\{(a - m_y) / (2b)\} [D2cb / (4b^2 - c^2)] \qquad (3.19)$$

Equation 3.19 can be simplified by assuming that the goods are perfect substitutes, that is, b = c.

$$X^f = \{2(a - m_x) / (2b)\} [2D/3] - \{(a - m_y) / (2b)\} [2D/3] \qquad (3.20)$$

$$X^f = \{(a - (2m_x - m_y)) / 2b\} [2D/3] \qquad (3.21)$$

Two key factors must now be considered: the role of asymmetric country size; and the role of asymmetric production costs, or "comparative advantage". Consider country size first and assume symmetric costs, $m_x = m_y$. Equation 3.20 reduces to:

$$X^f = \{(a - m_x) / (2b)\} [2D/3] \qquad (3.22)$$

The term in the braces is the autarky equilibrium output of X. Thus free trade increases the output of X — a sufficient condition for gains from trade if, and only if, $D > 3/2 = 1.5$; that is, if the foreign country is at least 50 per cent as large as the home country.

The reasoning behind this result is as follows. The opening of trade offers the home firm a larger market, which stimulates production. However, the home firm must also share that larger market with another firm, which works to reduce production. If the foreign market is exactly the same size as the home market, the home firm will increase production. While both firms could continue to produce the autarky output, each firm now perceives marginal revenue to be greater than marginal cost and will therefore increase output. This is a pro-competitive effect together with an implied decrease in average cost, a combination of the results shown in Figures 3.3 and 3.4.

Output will decrease if the foreign market is less than half of the size of the home market. The intuition can be seen by thinking about the foreign market being only 1 per cent of the size of the home market. In this case, the home firm gains a tiny amount of sales in the foreign market at the cost of a sizable loss of sales in its home market to its new rival, and output falls.

Assume now that the markets are the same size ($D = 2$), but that the home firm may have a cost advantage or disadvantage, $m_x \neq m_y$. This is a real cost comparison, in terms of good Y in each country. m_x and m_y denote the number of units of Y that must be given up in the two countries to produce a unit of X. This comparison therefore indicates Ricardian comparative advantage.

With $D = 2$, Equation 3.21 simplifies to:

$$X^f = (a - 2m_x + m_y) [2/(3b)] \qquad (3.23)$$

Compare this to the autarky output in (3.14):

$$X^f > X^a \quad \text{iff} \quad (m_x/m_y) < [(a/m_y) + 4] /5 \qquad (3.24)$$

Note that a, the intercept of the demand curve must be greater than m_y, the marginal cost, if any Y is to be produced. Thus, the minimum value of the right side of (3.24) is 1. Now, suppose that $a = 2m_y$. This constitutes the reasonable assumption that if only one unit of Y were available, a buyer would pay twice the marginal cost (not the average cost!) for it. Then the right side of expression 3.24 becomes $6/5 = 1.2$. The production of X will expand in free trade unless the producer of X has more than a 20 per cent cost disadvantage relative to the producer of Y. (Again, I emphasize that this constitutes a real comparative cost disadvantage in terms of good Y or, alternatively, in terms of labour — m_i is the slope of the production frontier in country i.)

Assume finally that the goods are imperfect substitutes, that is, $b > c$. Unfortunately, a good deal of calculation is necessary to obtain a clear qualitative result. From (3.19) it is apparent that a decrease in c holding b constant decreases the size of the (positive) first term, but that this also decreases the size of the (negative) second term. What can be seen from (3.19) is that the limit, as c goes to zero (the products are "independent"), is:

$$\text{Limit } c \to 0 \quad X^f = D(a - m_x) / (2b) > X^a = (a - m_x) / (2b) \qquad (3.25)$$

As the products become independent, this is a pure market-size effect $(D > 1)$ and so output must increase over autarky. Note also, that X^f in (3.25) is greater than X^f in (3.22), the equation for X when costs are the same in the two countries and the goods are perfect substitutes. In the limit, the decrease in c must increase X above its value at any finite level of c. The relationship between X^f and c is monotonic in (3.19), and thus a decrease in c increases X^f, irrespective of the initial cost or differences in country size.

Any reduction of substitutability effectively increases demand for each product faster than it increases effective market power due to reduced competition between the two products. It is apparent from the reaction functions in (3.17) that a decrease in c causes each firm to expand its output at the current output level of the other firm. Imperfect substitutability therefore works to counteract a country's possible disadvantage in being the high cost producer or the larger country by helping to expand output.

A numerical example has been chosen to emphasize the non-comparative advantage gains from trade. Suppose there are two absolutely identical countries. The populations are the same, as are the marginal costs of production for the producers of X and Y. X and Y are symmetric and perfect substitutes. These are essentially the conditions to illustrate gains from trade due solely to decreasing average cost and pro-competitive gains.

If the budget constraint expressed by (3.11) is substituted into the utility function of (3.10), and the equations for p_x and p_y are also substituted into that equation, a simple expression for welfare is obtained that is valid in either the condition of autarky or free-trade equilibrium (recall that C_i is consumption per capita).

$$U = (b/2) \, C_x^2 + (b/2) \, C_y^2 + cC_xC_y + 1 + PR_x / L \qquad (3.26)$$

Multiplying by L gives total utility, which is reported below. The first three terms give consumer surplus (CS), and so (CS + L) is the value of utility derived from factor income. Similarly, if p_x in the profit equation is replaced by the equilibrium expressions for p_x, profits will be calculated by the simple formulae:

$$PR_x^a = (b/L) \, (X^a)^2, \quad PR_x^f = (b/(L+L^*)) \, (X^f)^2 \qquad (3.27)$$

Table 3.1 sets out the parameters of the model and the results. It also illustrates several points made earlier. The first is that it is possible for two identical countries to gain from trade when there are increasing returns and imperfect competition. The domestic IRS good has a higher output and a lower

Table 3.1

A Cournot Duopoly Between Two Identical Countries

Parameters: $L = L^* = 400$, $a = 6$, $m_x = m_y = 1$, $b = 10$, $c = 10$, $F = 40$

Variable	Autarky	Free Trade
Utility	735	804.44
CS + L	525	622.22
PR_x	210	182.22
X	100	133.33
Y	0	133.33
C_x	100	66.66
C_y	0	66.66
$Z = C_z$	260	226.67
p_x	3.5	2.67
p_y	-	2.67
X/L_x	0.7142	0.76923

Utility index:	1.0945
Nominal income index:	0.9545
X output per worker index:	1.0771
Diewert/Morrison index:	1.1199
[prod][endow][tot] =	[1.1199] [1.0] [1.0]

price — and factor productivity is higher. However, the X output per worker does not capture all of the gain. Some of the gain is the pro-competitive effect of reducing the relative price of X, experienced as a fall in profits by the X industry.

The Diewert/Morrison index is off by about 27 per cent (the authors recognize that it need not be correct in this case). Nominal income has decreased but the only price change is negative (p_x falls and Y is used as numeraire). The B index discussed in the previous chapter (the price deflator), therefore, is less than one (0.85230 to be precise). The productivity index [A/(BC)] is greater than the increase in nominal income (C = 1) and, in this case, greater than the utility index. The terms-of-trade index [D/E] does not change since there is no trade initially; imports and exports have identical shares of income after trade, and the import price equals the price of the export good. The values of D and E are the same, so the index is one (because of the symmetry of the countries, there is no trade in Z).

The explanation as to why the productivity index, designed for a competitive, constant-returns economy, increases is not at all straightforward. In the competitive model, price and output changes must be positively correlated; in this case, they are negatively correlated. Consider Figure 3.3, showing an initial equilibrium at A and price ratio p^a. Under conditions of constant returns and perfect competition, the production frontier is tangent at A and the production frontier though A must lie "below" p^a (technically, p^a is supporting the production frontier). Thus, with constant returns, the new output point Q^1 in Figure 3.3 must lie outside the old production frontier. If, in the CRS/PC model, factor supplies have not changed, one must conclude that there have been technical change(s).

Not only is the index somewhat off, but if productivity is thought of in terms of technical change, the underlying change in the economy, as represented by the index, will be entirely misunderstood. This example demonstrates that industrial-organization-based changes in an open economy can appear as "productivity" changes in standard estimation. Again, there is nothing wrong with this, provided everyone recognizes that many different factors are combined in the estimate of "productivity".

In the previous section it was noted that an expansion in the output of the increasing-returns firm is a sufficient, but not a necessary, condition for gains from trade. Whether or not trade does result in such an expansion, however, remains an open question. In this section, a simple Cournot duopoly model was used to show that such an expansion will indeed occur provided that: the domestic firm does not have a large cost disadvantage; and the domestic country does not have a much larger domestic market. Disadvantages in these two areas can be offset if the goods are imperfect substitutes. In this model, however, it is difficult to generate an output contraction. One set of assumptions that yields such an outcome is that: the firm be at least 20 per cent less cost efficient (for a conservative estimate of (a/m_y)); the countries be the same size; and the goods be perfect substitutes.

This section tells a very different story from that told in the competitive chapter. Here, the output level of a firm has normative significance and since productivity measures are also directly tied to firm scale, productivity and real income move in the same direction. Policy should be concerned with whether or not domestic firms are competitive in the increasing returns sector, although this does not imply that the disappearance of the sector might not be welfare-improving as was shown in the previous section.

It is also true that an improvement in productivity in X (measured here as a reduction in m_x) might be better than an equal productivity improvement in Y (which would result in an increase in m_x). The increase in m_x because of increased productivity in Y production has adverse scale effects in X that partly negate the effects of the productivity increase. This does not imply that productivity should not be increased in competitive sectors. The possible perverse outcome is a simple application of the theory of the second best: since there is a distortion in the system (price exceeds marginal cost in X), an otherwise favorable change (a productivity increase in Y) might be harmful if it increases the size of the distortion, measured here as $(p_x - m_x) X$.

It has been demonstrated that measures of productivity can err in this type of model. It is therefore easy to misinterpret the cause of measured productivity changes if the terms of reference are constrained to CRS/PC considerations. Productivity is not synonymous with technology.

One interesting point emerges for Canada. It is often argued that Canada has difficulty competing because of its small market. By implication, small countries are less competitive. This chapter suggests, however, that the proposition may be back-to-front. If the free trade outcome is compared to the autarky outcome, it is the small country that reaps the major gains from free trade. This contention is a rigorous formulation of the arguments of Eastman and Stykolt and the Wonnacotts; small protected markets are inefficient, so free trade forces efficient scale — exit. Competitiveness is measured in this model by the relative sizes of the comparative cost coefficients, m_x and m_y, and certainly not by domestic market sizes. Further, in the presence of trade barriers, high-cost domestic production must not be taken as evidence that an industry will be non-competitive under conditions of free trade. With increasing returns and imperfect competition, cost competitiveness is endogenous.

Cournot Competition with Free Entry

The previous analysis has one serious flaw when it is applied to the majority of manufacturing industries. If one accepts the notion of profit maximization, one should also accept the notion of the entry of producers when profits are positive and exit when profits are negative. Statistical evidence, such as the data compiled by Baldwin and Gorecki, strongly supports the use of free-entry models in analyzing the manufacturing sector as a whole. This does not mean that there are no industries for which the oligopoly model is appropriate, however.

The analysis of gains-from-trade under free entry does not differ markedly from the analysis under no entry. However, the analysis of trade policy in some cases yields exactly opposite conclusions. Papers by Brander and Spencer, for example, focus on the oligopoly model and show the benefits of an activist industrial policy. Some of these conclusions are reversed under conditions of free entry and exit. The following section, will consider the free-trade versus the autarky situation. (Trade policy is discussed later.)

Let L and L* denote the labour forces and populations of the home and foreign countries respectively. Let subscript i denote the ith firm in the industry and X and Y (without subscripts) continue to denote total industry outputs. Assume domestic and foreign firms have the same costs. Let n_x and n_y denote the numbers of firms in the two countries. The profits of a firm in the X industry are given by:

$$PR_i = (a - bX / (L+L^*) - cY / (L+L^*)) X_i - mX_i - F \qquad (3.28)$$

Firms maximize profits by setting marginal revenue equal to marginal cost. This profit-maximization condition is given by:

$$a - b(n_x+1) (X_i / (L+L^*)) - cY / (L+L^*) = m \qquad (3.29)$$

Free entry drives profits to zero: price equals average cost. This condition is given by:

$$a - bn_x(X_i / (L+L^*)) - cY / (L+L^*) = m + F / X_i \qquad (3.30)$$

Equations 3.29 and 3.30, together with the two corresponding equations (not shown) for the foreign country, can be solved for the equilibrium output per firm and the number of firms. The autarky output per firm is obtained by setting Y and L^* both equal to zero. These outputs are:

$$X_i^a = [FL/b]^{1/2} \qquad X_i^f = [F(L+L^*)/b]^{1/2} \qquad X_i^f > X_i^a \qquad (3.31)$$

The larger market available through trade leads to an increase in the output per firm. The output increase is independent of different marginal costs and whether the goods are perfect substitutes.

Output also increases regardless of differences in country size, although the smaller the country, the larger the output increase per firm. Note a point made previously: the smaller country will have a smaller output per firm in autarky, and hence higher costs. However, higher costs do not necessarily mean techni-cal inferiority. Put another way, this cost difference does not mean that the firms in the small country will be disadvantaged in trade. Thus, the possibili-ties of losses from trade seem to disappear. Output expands with trade — a sufficient condition for gains from trade. Productivity also rises in both coun-tries, and rises more in the smaller country.

There is one exception, however — when the goods are perfect substitutes. In such a case, if the cost of the X and Y firms are unequal, the higher-cost firms will exit under conditions of free trade. The price will be equal to the average cost of the low-cost firms. Even in this case, however, the high-cost country gains from trade (again, bear in mind that the condition of expanded output is sufficient, not necessary, for gains). With no profits, the welfare change for each country is equal to consumer surplus change. The price to the high-cost country falls with trade, and the consumer surplus increases. The shut-down of the industry is clearly a loss of competitiveness according to some definitions, but it increases real income. It should be noted that this extreme result does not generally occur when there is more than one factor. Reducing output, as explained in the previous chapter, generates a reduction in the cost of the factors used intensively in the increasing returns sector, with the result that the industry can be competitive at a lower level of output.

It greatly simplifies exposition if goods are assumed to be perfect substitutes. Henceforth, therefore, let $b = c$, and therefore $m = m_x = m_y$. Also assume that $L = L^* = 1$ and $L + L^* = 2$. These assumptions make it possible to derive a simple comparison of the numbers of firms in the home country in autarky versus free trade.

$$n_x^a = (a - m) / (bF)^{1/2} - 1 \qquad\qquad (3.32)$$

$$n_x^f = (1/2) [(a - m) (2/bF)^{1/2} - 1] \qquad\qquad (3.33)$$

The formula shows that, provided $n_x^a > 1$, the result is:

$$n_x^f < n_x^a < 2n_x^f = n_x^f + n_y^f \qquad\qquad (3.34)$$

This equality follows from the symmetry in the model and shows an outcome similar to that discussed in connection with Figure 3.5. As a result of trade, there are fewer firms in each country individually, but there are more firms in total than existed in each country in autarky. Also, in each country fewer resources are used up in fixed costs, yet there is more competition.

The intuition behind the results on output expansion per firm and the exit of some firms has to do with perceived elasticity of demand. When trade is opened, each firm perceives demand to be more elastic and hence each firm increases output (marginal revenue is less than marginal cost at the autarky output). This causes the price of the good to fall, however, and since firms were making zero profits initially, some firms must exit to reestablish equilibrium.

Finally, it can be shown that total industry output increases in both countries; that is, output expansion per firm exceeds the contraction due to exit. The following derive from (3.31), (3.32), and (3.33):

$$X^a = (a - m) / b - (F/b)^{1/2} < X^f = (a - m) / b - (F/2b)^{1/2} \qquad\qquad (3.35)$$

$$X^f - X^a = (F/b)^{1/2} \left(1 - (1/2)^{1/2}\right) \qquad\qquad (3.36)$$

Industry output increases as fixed costs increase. Note that this is also true on a proportional basis, as shown by dividing (3.36) by X^a: the numerator increases and the denominator decreases with an increase in F.

It must be emphasized that the condition of production expansion refers to output per firm. If total industry output expands simply because of the entry of new firms at the old scale, then the industry production function behaves as if it has constant returns to scale, and there is no benefit. (This is an important condition in the policy analysis that follows.)

Table 3.2 presents a numerical example of free trade versus autarky for two identical countries when there is Cournot competition and free entry. The parameters are the same as those used in the duopoly example to permit easy comparison.

Utility rises 6.7 per cent as a result of trade. Output per firm rises 41 per cent and the number of firms falls from 4 to 3.03.

Note that the output of both X and Z increases, and that the total consumption of the goods $(C_x + C_y)$ increases. The situation is thus similar to that shown in Figure 3.5, where efficiency gains are taken in the form of increased consumption of both goods. Output per worker rises 17 per cent in the X and Y industries, and the Diewert/Morrison index rises by 12.9 per cent. The latter is double the true utility increase, and is therefore far off the mark. I can offer no explanation for this at present.

A comparison of Tables 3.1 and 3.2 yields some interesting results. Utility is higher under duopoly than under free entry. Free entry results in a lower

Table 3.2

Cournot, Free Entry Between Two Identical Countries

Parameters: $L = L^* = 400$, $a = 6$, $m_x = m_y = 1$, $b = 10$, $c = 10$, $F = 40$

Variable	Autarky	Free Trade
Utility	720	768.58
CS + L	720	768.58
PR_x	0	0.
X_i	40	56.57
n_x	4	3.03
X	160	171.72
Y	-	171.72
C_x	160	85.86
C_y	0	85.86
$Z = C_z$	80	106.86
p_x	2.0	1.71
p_y	-	1.71
X/L_x	0.5000	0.5858

Utility index:	1.0674
Nominal income index:	1.0000
X output per worker index:	1.1716
Diewert/Morrison index:	1.1290
[prod][endow][tot] =	[1.1290] [1.0] [1.0]

price for X due to added competition but resources are consumed as the fixed costs of the additional firms, effectively lowering the factor endowment left for actual output. In my example, an efficient monopolist is preferable to an inefficient competitive industry. I cannot defend the generality of this result, however, and I know of no formal theoretical analysis on this point.

As in the case of the duopoly model, there are gains from trade over autarky, (assuming, of course, that nothing that can go "wrong" in this model); a cost inefficient X industry could shut down, but there would still be welfare gains. Also, as in the case of the duopoly example, gains are larger for the smaller country since the expansion in output per firm is larger there. With the proviso that a small country has access to equivalent technology, I thus conclude that a small country is a major beneficiary of free trade in the industrial organization model.

Trade Policy

Since 1980, many papers have been written on the subject of trade policy with increasing returns and imperfect competition. (Although space considerations preclude a review here, I refer readers to works by Helpman and Krugman, 1985 and 1989.) My objective here is to consider the effects of trade policy by looking at several specific cases.

Earlier in the chapter, I discussed the importance of "output expansion by increasing-returns firms" in determining the gains from trade. It follows that trade policies are likely to have different effects from those derived from traditional analysis, depending on their effects on firm scale. Some policies that are welfare-reducing in the competitive model may be welfare-increasing if they have a sufficient positive effect on firm scale.

This can be shown by developing the analysis for a production subsidy on good X by the home country. In the competitive model, such a subsidy must be welfare-reducing if X is exported. It will be shown here that it can be welfare-increasing in the duopoly model. However, it will also be shown that such a subsidy is welfare-reducing in the free entry model, and that it promotes entry by additional firms rather than to the expansion of output by existing firms.

Consider first the duopoly and let the specific subsidy rate on output by denoted by s. The X producers profit equation corresponding to (3.15) and its reaction curve corresponding to (3.16) are now expressed as follows:

$$PR_X = (a - b(X/D) - c(Y/D)) X - m_X X + sX - F \qquad (3.37)$$

$$X = (a - m_X + s) / (2b/D) - (c/(2b)) Y \qquad (3.38)$$

The subsidy leads to a new equilibrium in which there is a larger output of X and a smaller output of Y. Note that the subsidy has exactly the same effect as reducing the marginal cost of X production. Assume that the marginal costs of both firms are the same and that the goods are perfect substitutes ($c = b$) and that the markets are the same size ($D = 2$). If m_x in (3.23) is replaced by ($m - s$), and similarly for the corresponding equation for Y, the following equilibrium outputs emerge:

$$X = (a - m + 2s) [2/(3b)] \qquad (3.39)$$

$$Y = (a - m - s) [2/(3b)] \qquad (3.40)$$

The subsidy increases X and total ($X + Y$), but reduces Y. There is therefore a positive firm-expansion effect in the home country and a contraction in the foreign country.

The effect on the foreign country is shown in Figure 3.7 (replace X on the horizonal axis with Y and Y with Z on the vertical axis) and the effect on the home country in Figure 3.8. In each case, A can represent the identical output bundles in free trade at free trade price ratio p^*. There is no net trade due to the symmetry of the countries (but there are gains from trade over autarky), so A can represent both production and consumption of X and Y. The subsidy

Figure 3.8

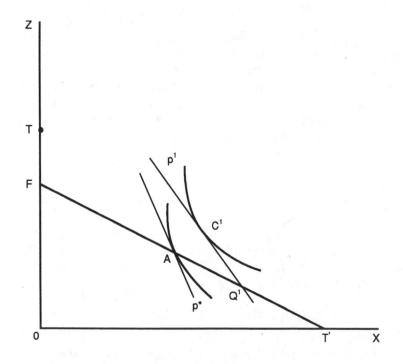

increases total world output as shown in (3.39) and (3.40), so the price ratio falls to p^1 with the subsidy. Home production occurs at point Q^1 in Figure 3.8 and consumption at point C^1. Figure 3.7 shows foreign production at Q^1 and consumption at C^1.

The home country gains and the foreign country loses as a result of the positive and negative production expansion conditions respectively. The loss in the foreign country is not inevitable, however, if it eventually ceases production. The price line rotates around point T in Figure 3.7 and eventually utility will improve over point A. These figures, therefore, depict a situation where a policy that is never optimal in terms of traditional CRS/PC trade theory is, indeed, welfare-improving.

Another interesting insight can be gained by writing the X producers total cost (TC) as TC = (AC)X where AC is average cost. The change in total cost can be written as:

$$d(TC) / dX = MC = (AC) + d(AC) / dX \tag{3.41}$$

The welfare effect $(p_x - MC)dX$ discussed earlier in the chapter can then be written as:

$$(p_x - MC)dX = (p_x - AC)dX - d(AC). \tag{3.42}$$

The first term represents the change in the X firm's profits and is sometimes referred to as the profit-shifting effect. The subsidy captures a larger share of world profits for the domestic firm. The second term also has a positive sign (it is minus a minus) when output increases (average cost falls) and represents the scale efficiency effect. In the present duopoly model, both effects are positive for the home firm and both are negative for the foreign firm.

Table 3.3 sets out an example of a subsidy s = 0.5 (half of marginal cost) to the home firm for the same parameter values as were used in the previous two examples. Foreign quantities are denoted with an *. Home utility rises by about 5 per cent and foreign utility falls to 98 per cent of its original value. Consumer surpluses rise in both countries since p_x falls, and there is a large profit gain in the home country and a large profit fall in the foreign country. Clearly, the latter is the source of the overall loss for the foreign country. The home firm's profit gain of 97.78 exceeds the subsidy bill of 80. Output per worker and the associated productivity measure increases in the home country (the second effect in equation 3.42) and falls in the foreign country. The Diewert/Morrison index is approximately correct for the home country and for the foreign country as well.

Both countries consume the same amounts of X and Y because of the income-inelastic demand formulation. Finally, the difference in utility is attributable to the difference in C_z.

Table 3.3

Cournot Duopoly with Specific Production Subsidy

Parameters: $L = L^* = 400$, $a = 6$, $m_x = m_y = 1$, $b = 10$, $c = 10$, $F = 40$ $s = 0.5$

Variable	Subsidy	Free Trade
Utility	845	804.44
Utility*	785	804.44
CS + L (both)	645	622.22
CS + L - sX	565	622.22
PR_x	280	182.22
PR_y^*	140	182.22
X	160	133.33
Y	120	133.33
C_x	80	66.66
C_y	60	66.66
Z	190	226.67
Z^*	240	226.67
C_z	250	226.67
C_z^*	200	226.67
p_x	2.5	2.67
p_y	2.5	2.67
X/L_x	0.80	0.77
Y/L_y	0.75	0.77

	Home	**Foreign**
Utility index:	1.0504	0.9758
Nominal income index:	1.0305	0.9275
X output per worker index:	1.0400	0.9750
Diewert/Morrison index:	1.0748	0.9664

$\qquad$ [prod] [endow] [tot] = [1.0748] [1.0] [0.9973]

$\qquad$ [prod] [endow] [tot]* = [0.9638] [1.0] [1.0027]

Now consider the same problem with free entry. From (3.31) it can be seen that the marginal cost of production does not enter the formula for the equilibrium output per firm. Firm scale is independent of the subsidy! (This result was first demonstrated by Horstmann and Markusen, 1985.) The outcome is even worse with an *ad valorem* subsidy on average cost or output; output per firm falls with the subsidy. This formal result verifies the theories of Eastman and Stykolt, and the early work of the Wonnacotts. Tariffs or, as in this case, a subsidy, can create inefficient entry of firms, inefficient scale, and welfare losses.

This situation is shown in Figure 3.9 where Q^0 is the initial free-trade production and consumption point at price ratio p^0 (again, there is no net trade initially, due to symmetry). p^0 is equal to average cost and therefore to the slope of the line connecting Q^0 and T. The subsidy does not lead to change in firm scale and therefore average cost, but to entry. The new production point in Figure 3.9 is at point Q^1 on the new production frontier TFT''.

In Figure 3.9, the price ratio falls by the amount of the subsidy, to p^1 and consumption is shown at point C^1. In this scenario the foreign country has been driven out of the industry (the result suggested earlier). Because the goods are perfect substitutes and there is only a single factor in play — labour — the "high cost" firms cannot compete.

The situation for the foreign country is shown in Figure 3.10, where Q^0 is the initial production and consumption point identical to Q^0 in Figure 3.9. The subsidy causes the foreign country to specialize in Z, producing at T as shown

Figure 3.9

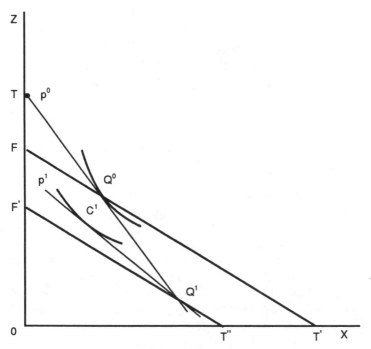

Figure 3.10

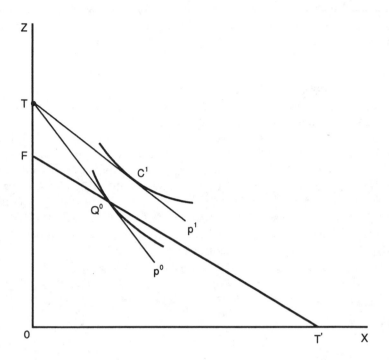

in Figure 3.10. Since the price of X has fallen, consumption rises to point C^1 and welfare unambiguously improves. Table 3.4 sets out a numerical example of the subsidy $s = 0.5$ using the same parameter values as those in the other Tables.

There was one interesting surprise in constructing this example. The demand for labour to produce the world's entire supply of X in the home country after the subsidy exceeded its endowment. I therefore have the home country contracting with the foreign country to import "guest workers". The earnings and the consumption of the migrant workers are included in the income and consumption of the foreign country in Table 3.4 for a valid welfare comparison. Utility for the home country shown in the Table is the utility of the original inhabitants.

In this case, the foreign country gains and the home country loses, which is exactly the opposite of the duopoly case. Both countries have an increase in consumer surplus, but the subsidy payments in the home country exceed the gain in consumer surplus so that welfare decreases. There are no profit effects, which were crucial in the duopoly example. The home country loss in utility is about 3.5 per cent; the foreign country gain is 2.1 per cent. It is not clear how

Table 3.4

Free Entry Model with Specific Production Subsidy

Parameters: $L = L^* = 400$, $a = 6$, $m_x = m_y = 1$, $b = 10$, $c = 10$, $F = 40$, $s = 0.5$

Variable	Subsidy	Free Trade
Utility	742.27	768.58
Utility*	784.87	768.58
CS + L (both)	859.43	768.58
PR_x	0	0
PR_y	0	0
X_i	56.57	56.57
n_x	6.78	3.03
X	383.43	171.72
Y	-	171.72
$C_x = C_x^*$	191.72	85.86
C_y	0	85.86
Z	0	106.86
Z^*	145.45	106.86
C_z	51.55	106.86
C_z^*	93.90	106.86
p_x	1.21	1.71
p_y	-	1.71
X/L_x	0.5858	0.5858

	Home	**Foreign**
Utility index:	0.9678	1.0212
Nominal income index:	0.7088	0.8149
X output per worker index:	1.0000	-
Diewert/Morrison index:	0.8723	0.9844

[prod] [endow] [tot]   = [0.9002] [1.0] [0.9691]

[prod] [endow] [tot]* = [0.9578] [1.0] [1.0278]

to calculate the Diewert/Morrison index in this case since some foreign labour is used in the home country to produce X. The index was calculated on the basis of national income, not national product, and thus includes in the foreign country's index that part of X production that their workers account for. This may not be standard practice, but I have not encountered any discussion of foreign ownership in the literature on productivity I have read to date. Calculating the index on the basis of national product would give a lower value for the home country and a higher value for the foreign country. However, this index underestimates the gain to the foreign country because most of the subsidy on all consumption of X (home and foreign) is paid for by consumers in the home country. There is no way for the index to pick up this effect.

The fact that the output per firm does not depend on marginal cost does not imply that there is no benefit to technical change that reduces this cost. This can easily be seen in Table 3.4 by supposing that the marginal cost of production has fallen by 50 per cent for "real" reasons. All of the output effect etc. are then exactly the same except that there are no subsidy payments in the home country. Welfare is thus expressed by the sum of (CS + L) = 859.43 — an 11.8 per cent increase in utility. Interestingly, the gains from the technical improvement are enjoyed equally by the two countries.

Much of the intuition behind the contrast of the free-entry and duopoly results can be obtained by examining (3.42). In the free-entry case, there are no profits so the first term is zero. There is also no change in firm scale so the second term is zero. Thus, there is no industrial-organization benefit from the production subsidy, and the subsidy is welfare-reducing as in a competitive, constant-returns model.

Other examples could be presented, but I believe the subsidy case serves to illustrate the reasoning behind many other results.

To summarize, in the increasing-returns, imperfect competition model, firm scale is an important welfare variable. Policies that expand firm scale can be welfare-improving (other things being equal). It is equally important to emphasize, however, that the welfare variable relates to firm scale, not industry scale. Therefore, policies that expand industry scale without expanding firm scale are welfare-reducing just as in the competitive model. (Of course, it has also been noted that real technical change is welfare-improving if it generates savings in excess of costs even though it does not affect firm scale.) In situations where entry is easy, this, unfortunately, requires that governments not offer general incentives but, rather, that they become involved in "targeting" subsidies (or related policy instruments) on individual firms. This is an unpleasant business, and it may be that no incentives are better than general incentives.

Multinationals, Technology Transfer, and the International Fragmentation of Production

Many books have been written on these topics, and it is therefore unnecessary to provide a comprehensive review here. As in the previous cases, my approach is to develop a simple model that captures some of the key points emphasized in the literature.

The basic consideration in the theory of the multinational enterprise has to do with why these corporations exist at all. If there are costs to doing business abroad, why then is a country not adequately served by imports or by the production of its own domestic firms? The question of foreign production is typically answered by the "tariff jumping" argument: firms produce abroad to avoid tariffs and/or transport costs. However, this does not explain why that production is executed by a foreign multinational enterprise (MNE) rather than a domestic firm. Suppose that technology is freely available everywhere, and that there are some costs to doing business abroad. A domestic firm would then always be able to undercut a foreign entrant and the production (supported by transport considerations or tariff barriers) would be executed by domestic firms.

A key to the answer is in the empirical literature. Studies have repeatedly concluded that the importantance of multinationals in an industry is highly correlated with variables such as:

• R&D expenditures as a percentage of sales
• professional and technical workers as a percentage of an industry's employment
• technical newness and sophistication of products
• advertising and other product-differentiation variables
• the age of the firm

(See, for example, Beaudreau, 1987, for a review and original firm-level empirical work; see also Caves, 1982.)

Such empirical work suggests the existence of what I call "knowledge-based assets" or "knowledge-based capital". Dunning calls them "ownership advantages"; Caves calls them "intangible assets", and another commonly-used term is "firm-specific assets".

There appear to be three reasons why MNEs are found in industries in which knowledge-based capital is important. (The situation is muddied by the fact that some of these industries are also intensive in the use of physical capital).

First, the services of knowledge-based assets — such as engineers and managers — are easily transported between distant locations while the services provided by plant and equipment generally are not.

Second, knowledge-based capital often has a joint-input or "public good" characteristic within the firm. Once engineers develop a blueprint for a new product or production process, that blueprint can be sent to any number of additional plants for essentially zero marginal cost. The blueprint is thus like a public good within the firm.

Third, the same public-good property means that the value of knowledge-based capital can be easily dissipated. Other firms can learn to produce the good or copy the process by having access to the blueprint just as can the firm's own branch plants. Due to the implied moral hazard and other agency problems, however, the firm may wish to transfer the asset internally through foreign direct investment (FDI).

The joint-input property of knowledge-based assets in turn gives rise to one form of what Eastman and Stykolt refer to as multi-plant economies of scale. Suppose that fixed costs come in two forms: firm-specific (denoted by F) and plant-specific (denoted by G). The firm-specific cost F is the R&D cost required to design a product or production process. Once this cost is incurred, F becomes knowledge-based capital (or intangible asset, or firm-specific asset) that can be supplied to any number of plants. G is the physical capital cost of plant and equipment that creates scale economies at the level of the individual plant. The total fixed cost invested by an industry consisting of two single-plant firms is (2F + 2G), while an industry consisting of one two-plant firm is (F + 2G). Multi-plant economies of scale thus arise in avoiding the costly duplication of firm-specific costs incurred by multiple single-plant firms.

Knowledge-based assets and the implied multi-plant economies of scale give rise to the principal motive for the existence of MNEs as equilibrium market structures. They also suggest a normative interpretation for the role of MNEs in improving world welfare. MNEs increase world welfare by creating and exploiting knowledge-based capital efficiently.

The other side of the normative coin is market power (as outlined in the previous three sections of this chapter). If one two-plant firm replaces two single-plant firms, technical efficiency will be purchased at the expense of altered market conduct and the concentration of more monopoly power. The trade off between the two determines not only total world welfare, but also the distribution of welfare between home and host countries.

This theory, which I believe is generally supported by the great weight of empirical evidence, has important implications for understanding the direction, composition and volume of trade. Consider the situation of an industry which has a single firm with one plant located in the home country and exporting to the foreign country. Compare this to the situation where this single home-country MNE maintains plants in both countries. In the first case, the home country exports X and imports Z. The only trade is in merchandise. In the case of the MNE, the R&D activity (F) may be conducted at home and some of the good may in fact be imported from the foreign country. What can be observed here is the trade of a good (X) for the services of firm-specific assets (F), such as management and engineering services. The trade account is now radically different. The home country has a deficit on the merchandise account and a surplus on the service account. Exports of management and engineering services are traded for imports of goods. This is essentially what is meant by "technology transfer" when it happens within the firm.

The normative implications of such a trade pattern may be misunderstood if X is a "high-tech" good whose production the government wishes to encourage. The trade performance statistics are compiled on the basics of the location of actual production; the "service" or "technology transfer" component of trade in the industry is ignored. When the domestic firm switches to FDI and imports the physical product, there is a deterioration of the trade balance in high-tech and a loss of competitiveness in this product is inferred. There is absolutely nothing wrong with this shift if, indeed, the object of interest is the R&D component and not the actual production phase of the industry. This is especially true since many of the actual manufacturing jobs in high-tech industries are, to the best of my knowledge, low-skilled, labour-intensive manufacturing jobs.

The possibility of importing the high-tech good can be argued more rigorously by considering an example that has more than one factor of production — a specific factor in Y will do. Applying resources to firm-specific costs requires the high-tech sector to draw more skilled labour away from other sectors, which drives up the home country's wage rate in relation to other countries. The firm will locate production internationally so that the marginal cost of physical production is roughly equal everywhere. This implies that if R&D and other headquarters activities are located at home, then a larger share of manufacturing employment will be located in low-wage countries relative to the home country.

The foregoing involves aspects of FDI, technology transfer, as well as trade in producer services. In my view these elements are more closely related than we realize. We underestimate the importance of trade in producer services because services transferred within an MNE are included under the present system of classification in the balance of payments as part of the payments for FDI. Arm's-length trade in producer services is classified as trade in producer services in another section of the service account. In view of this, I suggest that we are not only underestimating trade in producer services and technology transfer in a quantitative sense, we are also under appreciating it in the normative sense. The above example indicates that it is time to take a look at more than the direction and flow of physical goods when evaluating trade performance and competitiveness in high-tech sectors.

Figure 3.11 sets out an example consistent with earlier formulations for a host country. T is the maximum output of Z that can be produced. The distance TG in the diagram represents plant-specific fixed costs; the distance GF represents firm-specific fixed costs of beginning X production. TFT represents the production frontier if the country has a domestic firm that does its R&D and development work at home. Let the point Q^0 represent the autarky production and consumption point at price ratio p^0. Labour's income in terms of Y is given by the distance T, so labour's budget line is given by the line through T with slope p^0 as described earlier in the section on A Simple Model with Fixed Costs. Point C^1 in Figure 3.11 thus represents labour's consumption bundle and the difference between consumption bundle C^1 and production bundle Q^0 is consumption out of profits.

Figure 3.11 shows a case where the host country is worse off. If a foreign MNE were to enter the home country instead, the home country has the potential efficiency gain of saving F, shown by the movement of the production frontier to TGT". The vertical distance between the two production frontiers (FG in Figure 3.11) is the measure of the value of the technology or producer services transferred by the MNE to the host country. This is the positive side of the normative coin mentioned earlier. The other side is that the MNE may now capture profit gains that would otherwise go to domestic shareholders. With an income-inelastic demand for X, the MNE will choose the same output of X and produce at Q^1 in Figure 3.11. Workers will earn average cost and no profits will be captured in the domestic income stream. Thus consumption point C^1 becomes the point of total domestic consumption. The price has not changed and so there is no consumer surplus gain, only a loss of profits to foreigners.

In this example the foreign MNE does extremely well, capturing not only a return to its knowledge-capital ($Q^1 - Q^0$) — which theoretically cost it nothing to transfer abroad — but also the rents that were previously going to the domestic firm ($Q^0 - C^1$). This scenario should not be ignored. For example, the home market might not be sufficiently large to support two firms. If the MNE enters first, any potential domestic entrant is likely to be blocked and the MNE will continue to price in a monopoly fashion.

Figure 3.11

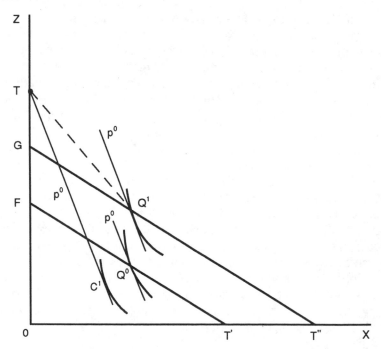

Figure 3.12 illustrates what is virtually an opposite scenario. Suppose, because of some unspecified condition in the industry, firms are forced to price at average cost. Referring to Figure 3.12, the autarky equilibrium is represented by point Q^0 at price p^0. Price equals average cost and there are no profits. On entry, the MNE is also forced to price at average cost (perhaps due to "severe" competition from other MNEs). Production occurs at point Q^1 and price ratio p^1. Again, there are no profits and so point Q^1 also gives the consumption bundle of the host country. In this case the country receives the technology or knowledge transfer as if it were free. Welfare improves accordingly.

A numerical example, in line with earlier ones, should follow at this point. There is a problem, however; with no trade barriers there is absolutely no motivation for FDI, so let us impose a specific tariff of t = 2 in both directions (T equals tariff revenue in Table 3.5 below). To generate a free-entry market structure with only one or two firms, it is also necessary to raise fixed costs from 40 to G = 20, F = 180. A one-plant firm incurs fixed cost of 200, while a two-plant firm incurs fixed costs of 220.

Table 3.5 retains the other parameters of the earlier examples. The goods X and Y are perfect substitutes, as before, and can both be referred to as X in order to avoid confusion. Four possibilities are considered. The first is an exporting duopoly where each country has one firm with one plant and each exports to the other coun-

Figure 3.12

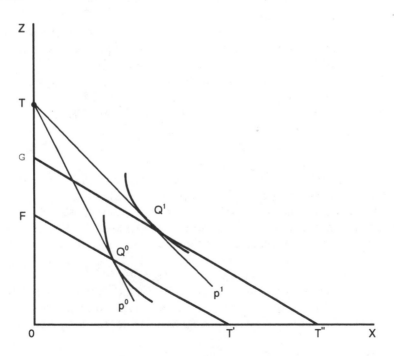

try. In the second case, the foreign firm buys out the home country firm for the profits that the latter was earning in the exporting duopoly and is then free to price as a monopolist. In the third example, the foreign firm does the same, except that it must pay the subsidiary half its monopoly profits.

In the second and third cases, I have also assumed that the foreign country imposes no duty on the imports brought in by its own firm's foreign subsidiary in the home country (a drawback provision). The location of the production of X is somewhat arbitrary. It would not be if there were another factor of production in Z (specific capital). In that case, the wage rates and marginal costs of X production would be equalized by dividing the cost of X production between the countries such that the level of Z production is the same in the two countries. I have done this in the example which, in turn, implies that the subsidiary in the home country exports X back to the foreign country. This is reminiscent of U.S. and Japanese multinationals locating production in Southeast Asia.

The fourth possibility is a multinational duopoly, where each national firm maintains plants in both countries. Again, it is assumed that there are no tariffs since firms are importing their own output in payment for export of technology/services and are thus assumed to qualify for drawback. Variables shown with the asterisk (*) denote the foreign country. The negatives of EX and EZ identify foreign imports of X and Y.

Referring to the column headed Export Duopoly, because of the high firm-specific fixed cost F, and the fact that the tariff is high in each country, the exporting duopoly is not very efficient. Each firm's exports to the other market are small (13.33) so there is little pro-competitive gain generated. The tariff significantly distorts consumption choice, so there is also a loss of consumer surplus. Profits of the firms are a modest 22.20.

The first Buy-Out column shows the outcome when the foreign firm buys out the home firm for its profits of 22.20. This reduces welfare in the home country, since the foreign firm can now charge the monopoly price. There is a loss in consumer surplus over the exporting duopoly, and there is no gain in profits. Similarly, there is a loss of consumer surplus in the foreign country, but a large gain in welfare due to the very large increase in profits. The MNE not only runs the plant in the home country for only the plant-specific cost of 20 instead of $(F + G) = 200$, but captures monopoly rents as well. The output per worker increases by 37 per cent over the duopoly situation. The saving of firm-specific costs substantially outweighs the anti-competitive contraction in X output. The trade flow is also interesting; the home country exports both X and Z to the foreign country as payment for the technology and as monopoly rent. The home country runs a trade account surplus to pay for its imported technology.

In the second Buy-Out column in Table 3.5, the foreign firm and the home-country subsidiary spit the rents, each receiving half the total monopoly profits of 280. In this case, both countries are better off compared to the ineffi-

Table 3.5

Alternative Market Structures

Parameters:
$L = L^* = 400$, $a = 6$, $m_x = m_y = 1$, $b = 10$, $c = 10$, $G = 20$, $F = 180$, $t = 2$

Variable	Export Duopoly	Buy-Out[1]	Buy-Out[2]	MNE Duopoly
Utility	591.07	547.20	665.00	624.43
Utility*	591.07	782.80	665.00	624.43
CS + L + T	568.87	525.00	525.00	622.22
Profit	22.20	22.20	140.00	2.21
Profit*	22.20	257.80	140.00	2.21
X	106.66	190.00	190.00	133.33[3]
X*	106.66	10.00	10.00	133.33[3]
EX	13.33	90.00	90.00	0.00
$Z = Z^*$	93.34	190.00	190.00	64.47
C_z	93.34	72.20	190.00	64.76
C_z^*	93.34	307.80	190.00	64.76
EZ	0.00	117.80	0.00	0.00
X/L_x (world)	0.348	0.476	0.476	0.377

Output per worker in X:
  MNE monoply/Export duopoly   =   1.3678
  MNE duopoly/Export duopoly   =   1.0833

[1] Foreign firm buys out home firm for latter's profits in the exporting duopoly.
[2] Foreign firm buys out home firm for half monopoly profits (280). When there is a foreign monopoly MNE (the buy-out cases), we assume production is located to keep Z production the same in both countries, see text.
[3] This is the firm's combined output from its two plants.

cient exporting duopoly. The savings of firm-specific costs of 180 outweigh the loss of consumer surplus due to the increased market-power distortion. In this case, the firm-specific costs are so large that the efficient monopoly is preferable to the inefficient duopoly by both countries. In both the monopoly outcomes, the home country produces 190 X while the foreign country produces only ten. The difference is the 180 units of labour used by the foreign country in firm-specific costs, meaning that both countries have the same total resources in the X industry and therefore produce the same amount of Z.

When profits are spit evenly, there is no trade in Z; the home country merely exports 90 units of X so both have a consumption level of $C_x = 100$ (the same as in the autarky equilibrium shown in Table 3.1). Again, the home country has a trade account surplus and the foreign country a trade account deficit. My earlier point is apparent in this example. It should not be concluded that the foreign country is "losing competitiveness" on the basis of its deficit in X production. The foreign country, indeed, has a surplus in the key element of high technology — the services of the firm-specific asset.

The last column shows the outcome of an MNE duopoly when each firm maintains plants in both countries. Profits (2.21) are just sufficient to support this market structure; slightly higher fixed costs would rule it out. The welfare levels are higher than the exporting duopoly, but lower than the second buy-out (monopoly) option. The MNE duopoly also has a higher consumer surplus than the latter, but the loss of profits due to the added burden of F outweighs the consumer surplus gain. Note that if F were small, the MNE duopoly would be preferred. The output per worker in the X industry is 8 per cent higher in the MNE duopoly than that in the export duopoly. Fixed costs are higher in the MNE duopoly by 20 for each firm (each firm has a second plant) but the higher output per firm due to the absence of a tariff inside the other's market more than offsets the added fixed costs.

Interestingly, it appears that the MNE duopoly is the Nash equilibrium market structure in this example. Operating within the exporting duopoly, each firm individually has an incentive to stop exporting and to open a branch plant in the foreign country due to the higher tariff. In this example, the home firm gains profits in the foreign market without losing profits in its home market. However, when they both chose in this fashion, they both make less profit in the MNE duopoly. This is the "prisoner's dilemma" of non-cooperative game theory and in this case it clearly works in favor of the consumers. Similarly, the monopoly outcomes will not be supported as equilibria if the firm and its subsidiary cannot prevent the entry of another firm. Thus the monopoly outcomes cannot be supported as representing a free-entry equilibrium. The MNE duopoly outcome can be supported because there is not a sufficient excess profit to allow a third firm to enter. The MNE duopoly is therefore the Nash equilibrium of the duopoly game. With somewhat higher fixed costs, the monopoly outcomes can be supported, and the division of rents becomes a bargaining problem.

To summarize, I have attempted in this section to show that the general outline of the increasing returns model can be extended to MNEs, FDI, and technology transfer when the existence of firm-specific fixed costs is recognized. Typically, these are thought of as arising from the existence of knowledge-based assets that are joint-inputs across plants. Such assets allow MNEs to exist despite costs of doing business abroad, and create efficiency gains from multi-plant production.

However, these may be purchased at the expense of increased market power. This creates an issue of welfare gains both for the world at large and the distribution of gains between home and host countries.

It is possible to construct situations where part of the rents captured by a foreign MNE go to a domestic entrepreneur in the absence of FDI, such that FDI makes the host country worse off. How empirically relevant such a result might be is not known. Finally, for the same reasons, a country gains when its MNEs have freer access to invest in the rest of the world. This spreads firm-specific costs over a larger output and encourages the firm to increase its R&D investments. In some cases, access to foreign markets may be crucial to survival. A final point is another caveat concerning trade performance: the role of trade in technology and producer services within the MNE must be taken into account as well as the physical flow of goods in assessing Canadian firms in high-tech industries.

Differentiated Final Goods, Specialized Intermediate Inputs, and Trade in Producer Services

Models with differentiated goods pose problems related to those above, but tend to work differently. The basic idea has already been discussed in connection with Figure 3.6. In that diagram, two goods (X and Y) are each produced with increasing returns or, more explicitly, a fixed cost and constant marginal cost. There are two "pure" models. First, the country can choose to produce both goods in autarky. Trade then allows each country to specialize in one of the goods with gains from trade captured in the form of lower average costs (more units of each good are produced from the given labour endowment). Second, the autarky equilibrium can, instead, have each country producing only one good in autarky, as represented in Figure 3.6. In this case, trade does not affect production (except that one country might switch products if both countries were producing the same one in autarky). Instead, the gains from trade are captured in the form of increased product diversity as consumers can now consume two different products.

Gains from trade are captured in both cases. In the case of increasing product diversity, no change in the scale of production is observed, but it is still true that the existence of scale economies are the cause of the gain from trade. Scale economies limit the number of goods produced in autarky and so they remain the cause of gains. Alternatively, it should be noted that with constant returns to scale and consumer tastes for diversity, a virtually infinite amount of product differentiation is possible, with each country producing an infinitely small amount of an infinit variety of goods. There are no gains from trade in such a world.

The existence of differentiated goods causes a problem for productivity analysis and real income index numbers as noted previously. The gains from trade may not appear in any measure of productivity at the level of the firm or industry. Similarly, because utility is not measured directly, the contribution to increases in utility by having smaller amounts of each of more goods is generally missed. Researchers are aware of this problem and Robert Feenstra and I have developed a GNP function for an economy with new goods.

Suppose that the consumer's utility function is given by:

$$U = [\,(sumX_i^{\,a})^{1/a}\,]^b\, Y^{1-b} \tag{3.43}$$

where the X_i is a set of differentiated products and Y is a homogeneous good produced by a competitive sector. Assume, too, that $0 < a < 1$, (i.e., the elasticity of substitution between two X_is is greater than one, implying that indifference curves touch the axis so not all varieties are necessarily consumed). If all varieties are produced in the same amounts, X can denote the output of a representative variety and n the number of varieties. The term in square brackets in (3.43) can then be expressed as:

$$[nX^a]^{1/a} = n^{1/a}X \quad 1/a > 1 \tag{3.44}$$

There are "increasing returns" to the number of varieties but constant returns to their levels. One unit of each of two goods yields more utility than two units of one good.

The cost of producing each variety includes a fixed cost F and a constant marginal cost M.

$$C_x = F(w) + M(w)X \tag{3.45}$$

where w is a vector of factor prices. The fixed costs limit the number of goods n that are produced in equilibrium. The demand function for an individual good is given by:

$$X_i = I^* / [\, p_i^{\,a}(sum\,\{p_i^{\,-ac}\})] \qquad c = 1 / (1-a) \tag{3.46}$$

where I^* is total expenditure on the differentiated goods.

Suppose now that there are many producers such that each producer views I^* and the sum of the cross-price effects in (3.46) as constant. Then the inverse elasticity of demand perceived by an individual producer is given by the simple expression (a-1) and marginal revenue is given by a simple mark-up on price.

$$MR = pa < p \tag{3.47}$$

The two equilibrium conditions, MR = MC and p = AC, are given by:

$$pa = M(w) \tag{3.48}$$

$$p = M(w) + F(w) / X \tag{3.49}$$

These equations express the output of a representative variety.

$$X = aF(w) / [(1-a) M(w)] \tag{3.50}$$

Suppose, for the sake of simplicity, that F and M use factors in the same proportion and that they are simply proportional to one another at any set of factor prices. Then (3.50) represents the special case where X is exactly constant.

$$X = [a / (1-a)] [F/M] \tag{3.51}$$

In this special case, all expansion and contraction of the economy is limited to the number of differentiated goods with no change in the levels of the outputs of the individual varieties. This then is a pure case much like that shown in Figure 3.6. The model has another interesting feature; it can be demonstrated that the amount of any good produced is exactly the socially optimal amount. However, there is still market failure due to scale economies. The number of goods produced in equilibrium is inefficiently small. Recall the production frontiers in Chapter 2, and suppose that the X axis measures the number of varieties produced, with parameters so scaled that exactly one unit of each variety is produced. An equilibrium is then described by a non-tangency between an indifference curve between Y and the X composite

$$[\operatorname{sum}(X_i^a)^{1/a}].$$

The relationship is expressed as MRT = pa < p. The price line (slope of the indifference curve) is steeper than the production frontier and differentiated goods are underproduced.

In this type of world, there are gains from trade in that each firm has an incentive to produce a uniquely different product, and consumers therefore have more choice with trade. It is also true that various trade policies that expand output of the sector are beneficial. Although subsidies and trade barriers add new firms without changing the scale of firms, the welfare effects are actually similar to those in the duopoly model developed above and are not like the free-entry model, which the present case appears to resemble. In the free entry model with a homogeneous output, the level of industry output itself is of no special significance; the benefits came from expanding output per firm. In the differentiated products model with constant output per firm, industry output itself has welfare significance and industry output is too low in the free market equilibrium, at least in the version of the model developed here. So, although there is free entry and zero profits, expanding industry output is nonetheless beneficial.

Exactly the same arguments can be put forward with respect to specialized or differentiated intermediate inputs into industry. (I have more to say about this in the next chapter, so my comment here is very brief.) Simply interpret U in (3.43) as output of some final good, Y, as the input of primary factors, and the X_i as differentiated intermediate inputs. Equation (3.44) shows that there are increasing returns to the "division of labour", but (3.45) implies that the division of labour is nonetheless limited by the extent of the market.

The intermediate-goods formulation is similar to that of the final-goods case, with some differences discussed in the next chapter. In this formulation, free trade is important to the efficiency of many final goods producers. Access to specialized intermediate inputs, which are prohibitively costly to develop at home, may be vital to efficiency. Among these inputs are producer services, such as management and engineering consulting, finance, and marketing services. Trade in these items (services) has traditionally been more restricted than trade in goods, since trade in service impinges on areas of immigration and foreign investment restrictions. Protection of these sectors of the Canadian economy may be unwise since the size of the economy cannot support a full range of specialties. Higher efficiency in the realm of production of final goods therefore calls for free trade in producer services.

A final comment concerning productivity and competitiveness measures is appropriate at this point. Gains from increased product diversity in final goods are difficult to measure and are certainly not picked up in productivity measures focussed on production. It is also likely that they are not picked up in measures of real income, either. However, since the same problem occurs more or less to the same extent across all the industrialized countries, the issue should not affect international comparison unduely. Increased division of labour embodied in more specialized intermediate inputs should, however, be picked up by standard productivity measures. Indeed, it would be interesting to try to separate this source of increased productivity from scale effects and technical change. This has not been done, so it remains an ambitious empirical question to be addressed.

Conclusions and Empirical Observations

This chapter presents a dramatically different view of the world from that described in the preceding chapter. Perhaps the most important difference is that in the industrial-organization world of scale economies and imperfect competition, the level of firm output has a direct bearing on some key concepts. First, productivity in the industrial-organization model is directly related to firm scale, whereas in the competitive model it is only related when a change in output is due to technical change. Here, a change in firm scale due to price or competitive conditions directly affects measures of total factor productivity. Second, real income is directly related to firm scale, as incremental units of output produce a welfare gain of price minus marginal cost.

These considerations also have a bearing on the competitiveness question. Measuring competitiveness in terms of either changes in productivity or trade performance may have a direct link to real income. One major caveat to the notion is that for the link to be valid improvements in trade performance must be due to changes in firm scale, not industry scale. I emphasized several times that firm and not industry output is the relevant real-income and real-productivity variable. Expansion in output as a result of the entry of new firms at the existing output level has no real income or productivity implications.

A second major caveat is to recognize that a country such as Canada cannot be a large player in all industries. In this connection it was shown that exit from an industry altogether often implies welfare gains. I suggested that the best response to trade is increased specialization, with some firms and industries expanding and others closing down. The worst-case scenario is to pursue an industrial policy that encourages excessive diversification of production at the cost of small scale.

A third caveat relates to differentiated final goods. In many cases, the gains from trade may be taken in the form of a greater variety of goods at no increase in output per firm. These gains are nonetheless due to scale economies which limit the number of goods in the first place, but such gains do not show up in productivity analysis and in all likelihood do not appear as part of real income index numbers either.

A fourth caveat relates to multinationals. With MNEs operating on the basis of knowledge-based assets, the location of physical production is not a reliable indicator of productivity or real income. Foreign MNEs may add to production within our country, but they also shift profits out that are the return to their firm-specific assets. Conversely, Canadian MNEs may shift production of standard, low-wage, labour-intensive activities abroad, which suggests a loss of competitiveness when the industry is evaluated by the location of physical production rather than by the location and import/export of skilled managerial and technical services.

It has been shown that the implications of these considerations for public policy depend very much on the conditions of entry and exit into an industry. When such opportunities are sharply limited, policies to stimulate an industry generally fall directly on firm output, and therefore on productivity and on real income. When entry is easy, these measures may simply generate expansion by attracting new entrants as in the case of the production subsidy. In such a situation, policy makers must make a choice in industrial policy sectors between doing nothing, offering general incentives, and targeting individual firms or industries. The subsidy example with free-entry suggests that there are cases where general incentives may be worse than doing nothing, even though the market equilibrium is not efficient. No one particularly likes the thought of targeting specific firms and industries, but experience in Scandinavia suggests that some success can be achieved using this approach.

Recent studies suggest that Canadian firms have responded well to trade liberalization, thus giving support to the general models and views presented in this chapter. Papers by Baldwin and Gorecki referenced at the end of this study certainly support the view that trade liberalization has led Canadian firms to rationalize the length of production runs and the number of products per firm. Admittedly, there has been net exit as a consequence of trade liberalization, but there has not been a contraction of employment. Thus, the evidence suggests an outcome similar to that shown in Figure 3.6, where increases in scale outweigh net exit and the industry expands. The new study by Caves (1990) strongly supports and adds to these findings. Tough international competition has led to the rationalization of Canadian industry not to contraction.

The papers by Baldwin, Gorecki, McVey and Crysdale (BGM&C) deserve special mention. Their studies use a comprehensive firm-level data set for the years 1970 and '79. Canadian tariffs fell by 30 per cent from 1966 to 1979 so their data allow for one observation on the actual (as opposed to counterfactual) effects of tariff reduction on plant size, product diversity, total numbers of firms, etc. BGM&C reported that between 1970 and 1979 both exports and imports (measured as a percentage of domestic trade) increased by about 20 to 25 per cent. The manufacturing sector cannot be easily classified as exporting or import competing; it does both, and in large amounts. This is consistent with the product differentiation version of our models.

BGM&C reported that the size of Canadian plants was small relative to U.S. plants, but that Canadian plant size increased by about 33 per cent between 1970 and 1979. Again, this is consistent with the pro-competitive and average-cost effects discussed above. They also reported a sizeable amount of entry and exit during this period. Of an industry's total sales in 1979, on average 16.2 per cent were accounted for by firms that entered (14 per cent) or took over existing plants. Firms that exited before 1979 by scrapping plants accounted for 25 per cent of 1970 sales. If divestiture is also counted, exit was 30 per cent of 1970 sales. This evidence strongly supports the free-entry model developed above. Baldwin and Gorecki's more recent paper (1990) reinforces this view and gives the role of entry and exit new empirical importance as a channel for industry adjustment and productivity growth.

Using a multiple regression analysis, BGM&C showed that high-tariff, high-concentration industries were initially significantly less efficient than other industries. Tariff reductions resulted in strong rationalizations rather than disappearances in these industries. They showed that in industries with high tariffs and high concentration, production runs were shorter and product diversity was higher for a given size plant than elsewhere in the manufacturing sector. From 1974 (the first year with data on a product basis) to 1979 BGM&C also found that the length of production runs increased and product diversity at the plant level decreased. This evidence strongly supports the predictions of the industrial organization model, especially the free-entry version developed above.

Counterfactual experiments using computable general-equilibrium models — such as the pioneering work of Harris and Cox (1984) and subsequent work by Markusen and Wigle (1989) — strongly concur. Free trade is estimated to increase the size of the manufacturing sector marginally, with strong effects on rationalization and productivity. Using the same models and imposing constant returns to scale generates much smaller gains from trade liberalization.

Much of the estimated adjustment to free trade in both the factual and the counterfactual studies occurs within individual firms and industries. This also supports the industrial-organization approach. The traditional competitive model suggests much more inter-sectoral adjustment with much higher associated adjustment costs. Lower cost adjustment within the manufacturing sector appears to be the actual outcome of liberalization. In my view, there is considerable evidence consistent with the broad outline of the industrial-organization approach developed in this chapter, particularly the free-entry version. I know of no evidence that directly contradicts this approach.

Research & Development, Education, Externalities and Dynamic Comparative Advantage

Introduction

This chapter deals with several topics, all of which are closely related, at least in an analytical sense. As in previous chapters, my approach is to develop one relatively simple example and then to apply it to specific issues. Most of the technical baggage needed to proceed has already been developed in the previous two chapters. The techniques used here draw on both the analysis of the competitive model and the analysis of the industrial-organization model, particularly the section on the gains-from-trade theorem and the section on differentiated products.

The point is that in the presence of various broadly defined externalities, market equilibria are not efficient. As seen in the previous case, trade and policies to promote or restrict trade will have additional effects depending on whether or not they expand or contract distorted sectors. Several examples will show that it is important to correctly identify the nature of the problem in designing public policy. In the open economy, a careful distinction must be maintained between domestic and trade policies, and policies focussing on production versus consumption.

The next section presents a basic general-equilibrium model of externalities followed by a discussion of the gains from trade. The remaining sections deal with the applications of the model in four situations: 1) complementary intermediate goods and services, 2) education and training, 3) research and development, and 4) dynamic comparative advantage.

A Simple Competitive Model with Production Externalities

This section sets out a simple model that develops the basic structure and the underlying theory of the general production externality problem. Although the model is widely used, it should probably be credited to Kemp (1969). As in Chapter 2, a two-sector model with goods X and Y will be considered. X represents the sector with externalities and since there is little interest in factor markets, V denotes a vector of factor supplies. Subscript i denotes the ith firm, and variables without subscripts denote total industry supplies.

Let the production function for the ith firm be:

$$X_i = (X^b) F_i (V_i) \qquad 0 < b < 1. \tag{4.1}$$

Output of the ith firm depends not only on its own private inputs V_i but also on total industry output X. b indicates the strength of the externality, with b = 0 implying no externality. It is assumed that the firm production functions have constant returns to scale and are identical across firms, so the i subscript on F can be dropped. It is assumed that individual firms are small relative to the market, so they view total industry output X as fixed. The private marginal product of factor j for an individual firm is then:

$$MP_j = (X^b) F_j \tag{4.2}$$

where F_j denotes the partial derivative of F (common to all firms) with respect to factor j. Since F has constant returns to scale, industry output can be determined simply by summing (4.1) over all the firms.

$$X = (X^b) F (V) \text{ implying } X = [F (V)]^c, \ c = 1 / (1-b) \tag{4.3}$$

The coefficient c thus indicates the degree of return to scale for the industry ($c \geq 1$). Note that c = 1 (constant returns) when b = 0.

Differentiation of (4.3) gives the industry or "social" marginal product of

V_j, denoted by MP_j^*.

$$MP_j^* = c[F(V)]^{c-1} F_j \qquad c-1 = b / (1-b) = bc \tag{4.4}$$

If (c-1) in (4.4) is replaced with bc, it can be seen from the second equation of (4.3) that (4.4) can be expressed as:

$$MP_j^* = c [F(V)]^{bc} F_j = c (X^b) F_j = cMP_j > MP_j \tag{4.5}$$

The social marginal product of a factor exceeds the private marginal product of that factor. Individual firms do not take into account the positive externality that they bestow on other firms when they increase output.

The marginal rate of transformation along the efficient production frontier is given by the ratio of the social marginal products of any factor j in the X and Y industries.

$$MRT = MP^*_{jy} / MP^*_{jx} \qquad (4.6)$$

Let $p = p_x/p_y$ be the price of X in terms of Y (Y is numeraire) as seen previously. The competitive equilibrium condition is that the value of the private marginal product of factor j is the same in the two industries.

$$pMP_{jx} = MP_{jy} \qquad (4.7)$$

Private and social marginal products are assumed to be the same in the Y industry. Substitute $(1/c)\ MP^*_{jx} = (1-b)MP^*_{jx}$ in place of MP_{jx} in (4.7). Combining this with (4.6) gives:

$$p\,(1-b) = MP^*_{jy} / MP^*_{jx} = MRT < p \qquad (4.8)$$

In market equilibrium, the price ratio is not tangent to the production frontier. This result is shown in Figure 4.1, where A is assumed to be the autarky

Figure 4.1

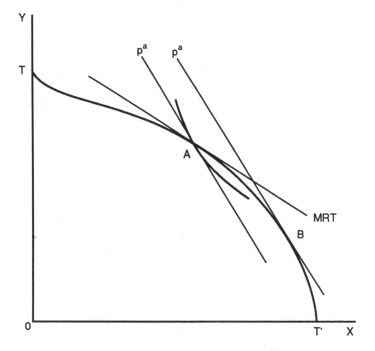

production and consumption point at autarky price ratio p^a on the production frontier TT'. The "wedge" between the price ratio and the MRT is (1-b), which goes to zero as b approaches zero, that is, as the industry production function approaches constant return to scale. The market equilibrium is not Pareto efficient, and X is under produced in that equilibrium. Once again, the reasoning is that firms do not consider the positive externality they have on other firms when they choose outputs, nor is there any mechanism for them to do so when there are many firms.

A second set of issues revolves around the shape of the production frontier. It was seen in the previous chapter, although the issue was not discussed in a technical sense, that the production set for the increasing returns economy was not convex; that is, the pattern described by the set of feasible production points was not convex. In Figure 3.1, for example, points between A and T (i.e., convex combinations of A and T) are not feasible production points. On the other hand, it was shown in Chapter 2 that differences in factor intensities in the multi-factor economy tended to "bow out" the production frontier (the production set is strictly convex).

In this chapter, both considerations are present at the same time. There is, therefore, a tension between scale economies and factor intensity effects. For many common functional forms, the production frontier develops a shape similar to that shown in Figure 4.1 by TT'. The production frontier is a convex function (the production set is non-convex) in the neighborhood of zero production of the increasing-returns good and becomes concave (the production set becomes locally convex) for larger values of output for the increasing returns sector. This is not a minor technical point, but rather is extremely important for questions of multiple equilibria and, by implication, for the gains from trade.

Multiple Equilibria and the Gains from Trade

The previous chapter noted that a sufficient condition for gains from trade is that the value of free-trade consumption exceed the value of autarky consumption when evaluated at free-trade prices.

$$p^f C_x^f + C_y^f \geq p^f C_x^a + C_y^a. \tag{4.9}$$

The balance-of-payments condition in free trade and the autarky market-clearing conditions are given by:

$$p^f C_x^f + C_y^f = p^f X^f + Y^f, \quad C_x^a = X^a, \quad C_y^a = Y^a \tag{4.10}$$

Substituting (4.10) into (4.9) then gives a sufficient condition for gains from trade based on production.

$$p^f X^f + Y^f \geq p^f X^a + Y^a.$$ (4.11)

This condition is always satisfied in a competitive, constant returns, distortion-free economy. The reason for this is that in such an economy, the production sector selects a point such that the price ratio is "tangent" to the production frontier (tangent is in quotes here because the concept must be generalized for corner solutions where some goods are not produced). Second, because the production set is convex, all other feasible production points lie below the price line through the equilibrium production point. That is, the free-trade production point maximizes the value of production at free trade prices. Condition 4.11 must hold.

The two conditions that ensure the sufficient condition (4.11) is satisfied-may be referred to as the "tangency condition" and the "convexity condition". What is evident, as depicted in Figure 4.1, is that it is not certain that either of these conditions is satisfied in an economy with positive production externalities. The production set may not be convex, and the price line (hyperplane in many dimensions) is not tangent to the production frontier (production surface). In Figure 4.1, the market equilibrium point A does not maximize the value of production at price p^a. That occurs at point B.

Now, consider Figure 4.2 with an autarky equilibrium at point C^0 with

Figure 4.2

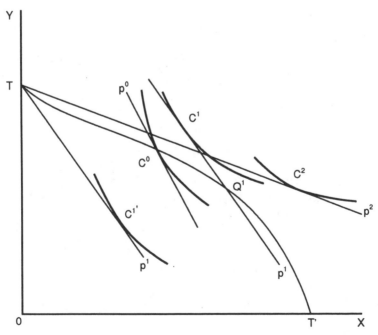

price ratio p^0. Suppose the world price ratio is $p^1 < p^0$. There may be multiple equilibria, such as the two shown in Figure 4.2 (there is generally a third, which is unstable). In one equilibrium, production occurs at point Q^1 and consumption at C^1; in the other, the economy specializes in Y and produces at T, consuming at C^3. This suggests something that was seen in the previous chapter: when an industry's output is less than the optimal amount in the autarky equilibrium, a further decrease in output due to trade may imply negative gains from trade, while an increase in output is sufficient. It can be shown that this is indeed correct, emphasizing again that the output-expansion condition is sufficient, not necessary. At price ratio p^2 in Figure 4.2, the country consumes at point C^2 and clearly gains from trade.

Let the economy's total factor endowment be denoted V, so $V = V_x + V_y$. Let w^f denote the vector of free-trade factor prices, so $w^f V$ (the sum of factor prices multiplied by their quantity) is the value of factor payments in free trade. This sum can be broken down in either of two ways.

$$w^f V = w^f V_x^f + w^f V_y^f = w^f V_x^a + w^f V_y^a \qquad (4.12)$$

Subtract the first breakdown from the left side of (4.11) and the second breakdown from the right side of (4.11). The sufficient condition for gains from trade is then:

$$(p^f X^f - w^f V_x^f) + (Y^f - w^f V_y^f) \geq$$
$$(p^f X^a - w^f V_x^a) + (Y^a - w^f V_y^a) \qquad (4.13)$$

With pricing at average cost, the left side of this inequality is always zero. This reduces the condition for gains from trade to:

$$(p^f X^a - w^f V_x^a) + (Y^a - w^f V_y^a) \leq 0. \qquad (4.14)$$

The second term is less than or equal to zero. The autarky factor input vector is cost minimizing at autarky prices, but not at free trade prices. Since competition minimizes costs, this in turn implies that using autarky inputs at free-trade prices generates a cost in excess of revenues, so that this term for the Y industry is less than or equal zero. The sufficient condition for gains from trade then reduces to only:

$$(p^f X^a - w^f V_x^a) \leq 0. \qquad (4.15)$$

If X^a is factored out, this can be written as:

$$(p^f - w^f V_x^a / X^a) X^a = (p^f - AC_x^{fa}) X^a \leq 0, \qquad (4.16)$$

where AC_x^{fa} is the average cost of producing the autarky output at free-trade factor prices. In a constant-returns world, this condition will hold, because the autarky input combinations are not the most cost-effective way to produce X^a at free-trade factor prices. This average cost therefore exceeds price and the left side of (4.16) is less than or equal to zero. Suppose, however, that the autarky output of X is higher than the free-trade output, $X^a > X^f$. Then with increasing returns to scale, the average cost of the autarky output may be less than the p^f, even when evaluated at free-trade factor prices. Thus (4.16) may fail when free-trade output of X is smaller than the autarky output. Again, expansion in X output is a sufficient (but not necessary) condition for gains from trade.

Before examining specific cases, three important differences between the externality model and the industrial-organization model of firm-level scale economies should be discussed. First, in the industrial-organization model (except in the differentiated products version) the markup of price over marginal cost is endogenous, depending on the degree of competition. One source of gains from trade is the pro-competitive gain where this margin shrinks. In the present model this gap is determined by technology: $p(1-b) = MC \leq p$. It does not disappear, or even shrink, with free trade. It is not, therefore, an analog of the pro-competitive effect.

Second, the problem of firm versus industry output does not exist here as it did in the industrial-organization model. The important welfare and productivity variable here is assumed to be industry output. There should be no concern about inefficient entry and, other things being equal, any policy that stimulates industry output is welfare-improving.

The third difference involves the issue of whether or not the externality is strictly "national" or "international" in scope. In the section on A Simple Competitive Model, it was assumed that X in (4.1) is the total domestic industry output. But what about in free trade? The gains from trade analysis of this section and those shown in Figure 4.2 assume that the domestic industry output continues to be the relevant variable. This is analogous to the oligopoly model in the last chapter where scale economies were internal to the single domestic firm. But might not the same inter-firm externalities extend to relationships among firms in partner countries? Perhaps not, if the externalities involve close physical contact, but it is difficult to imagine that this might be true among Canadian firms and not between Canadian and U.S. firms. If the externalities are within an international industry, then Figure 4.2 radically misrepresents the autarky versus free-trade situation and significantly underestimates the gains from trade. With trade, the production frontier moves out in proportion to X production as $(X + X^*)$ replaces X in (4.1) (X^* is foreign output).

Finally, regarding Figure 4.2, measured productivity will be higher at Q^1 than at C^0 which, in turn, will have higher measured productivity than at T (specializing in Y). Consider the Diewert/Morrison index comparing C^0 with

Q^1. The value of Q^1 is greater than the value of C^0 measured at either p^0 or at p^1. Thus, both the Laspeyres and the Paasche indexes will be greater than one comparing Q^1 over C^0. The Diewert/Morrison productivity index [A / (BC)] is the geometric mean of these two, and must therefore be greater than one.

In comparing autarky equilibrium C^0 and free-trade equilibrium Q^1, it can be concluded that productivity has increased, as in the case of the industrial-organization model with internal scale economies. This does not happen in the competitive model since, with the price line tangent to the (concave) production frontier, the Laspeyres index will be less than one while the Paasche index will be greater than one (the value of autarky production at autarky prices is greater than the value of free-trade production at autarky prices, hence the Laspeyres index is less than one).

In the competitive model, a price change does not register as a productivity increase in a properly constructed index. In the externalities model, however, it will do so, with an increase in industry output registering as an increase in productivity and conversely a decrease in output (as in equilibrium at T in Figure 4.2) registering as a reduction in productivity.

Complementary Inputs

One source of external economies is the existence of complementary inputs, the owners of which are not able to capture fully the benefits they confer on other producers. This notion was first developed by Ethier (1982) and I follow his formulation here. Suppose that X can be produced with varying degrees of specialization among intermediate inputs. Two specialized machines can be substituted for two general purpose machines, or two specialized engineers substituted for two engineers, each of whom knows a little about everything. Assume that the final good X is assembled only from these intermediate inputs, denoted S. Ethier uses a CES function much like the utility function in the differentiated goods section of the previous chapter.

$$X = [\text{ sum } (S^b)]^{1/b}, \quad b < 1. \tag{4.17}$$

As with the differentiated goods, assume that there is a design or other start-up cost such that an intermediate input is produced with a fixed cost $F(w)$ and a constant marginal cost $M(w)$. All intermediates have the same cost function and since they enter (4.17) symmetrically, any input produced is produced in the same amount. The cost function for a representative S is given by:

$$C = F(w) + M(w) S \tag{4.18}$$

Given symmetry, the output of the final good can be written as:

$$X = n^{1/b} S \tag{4.19}$$

where n is the number of specialized intermediate inputs. There are constant returns to the levels of the S, but increasing returns to n, the "division of labour". More specialization among the inputs is productive, but fixed costs limit the degree of specialization. We can also think of b as indicating the degree of complementarity among the S. When $b = 1$, $X = nS$ and the intermediates are perfect substitutes. There is no gain from increased specialization.

The price an S producer receives is the value of the marginal product of another unit of his good in final output. Denote this price as p_s with p continuing to denote the relative price of X, the final output.

$$p_s = p\,(1/b)\,[\,\text{sum}\,(S^b)\,]^{1/b-1}(bS^{b-1}) = p\,[\,\text{sum}\,(S^b)\,]^{1/b-1}(S^{b-1}) \qquad (4.20)$$

The revenue earned by the S producer is $p_s S$. Suppose that each S producer is so small that each views p and the summation term in square brackets in (4.20) as fixed. Denote this term as $[S^*]$. Revenue (R) and marginal revenue (MR) are then given by:

$$R = p\,[\,S^*\,]\,S^{b-1}S = p\,[\,S^*\,]\,S^b, \quad MR = pb\,[\,S^*\,]\,S^{b-1} \qquad (4.21)$$

However, recalling the definition of S^*:

$$MR = pb\,[\,S^*\,]\,S^{b-1} = pb\,(n^c)\,S^{1-b}\,S^{b-1} = pbn^c \quad c = 1/b - 1 \qquad (4.22)$$

Now, note from the equation on the right side of (4.20) that the price of an S, p_s, is given by:

$$p_s = p\,[\,S^*\,]\,S^{b-1} = p\,(n^c)\,S^{1-b}\,S^{b-1} = pn^c \qquad (4.23)$$

Taking (4.22) and (4.23) together with the cost function (4.18), gives the two conditions $MR = MC$ and $p = AC$ that solve for the two variables S, the output levels per intermediate, and n the number of intermediates or the "division of labour".

$$pbn^c - M(w) = 0 \qquad (4.24)$$

$$pn^c S - M(w)S - F(w) = 0 \qquad (4.25)$$

Replace pn^c in the second equation with $M(w)/b$ from the first and solve the two equations for S.

$$S = [\,b/(1-b)\,]\,F(w)\,/\,M(w) = [\,b/(1-b)\,]\,F/M \qquad (4.26)$$

where the second equality follows if it is assumed that F and M use factors in the same proportion and hence the ratio F/M is independent of factor prices. Equation (4.26) shows that the output of any S produced is constant, and so the industry expands solely as a result of the creation of more specialized intermediate inputs.

Finally, combine (4.23) with (4.24).

$$p_s b = M(w) < p_s. \tag{4.27}$$

This shows that the price of a unit of S is marked up over marginal cost by b. In turn, this implies that the relative price of X is a markup of b over marginal cost in terms of Y.

$$p > pb = MRT. \tag{4.28}$$

This creates an equilibrium point such as A in Figure 4.1, with the wedge between p and the MRT going to zero as b approaches one (the intermediates are perfect substitutes). It is thus clear that the source of the externality is the complementarity among the s inputs which cannot be internalized by the firms. When an additional firm enters, it confers benefits on the existing producers of S which the entering firm cannot capture. Also note the similarity of this result to (4.8) with b in the latter replaced by (1 - b) here. A high value of b (high scale economies) in the external economies formulation, is equivalent to a low b (high complementarity) here.

Now consider the industry cost function for X. This cost function is expressed as C (w, X) and is equal to the total costs of the intermediate inputs.

$$C (w, X) = nSM (w) + nF (w) \tag{4.29}$$

Replacing SM (w) with $[b/(1-b)] F (w)$ from (4.26) gives:

$$C (w, X) = n [F(w) / (1-b)] \tag{4.30}$$

But $X = n^{1/b}S$, so $n = X^b [((1-b)/b) (M/F)]^b$

Substituting this into (4.30) gives:

$$C (w, X) = c(w)X^b = \{ [F (w) / (1-b)] [((1-b)/b) (M/F)]^b\} X^b \tag{4.31}$$

such that $c(w) = \{ \ \}$. The function $c(w)$ is a standard unit cost function, homogeneous of degree one in factor prices. Note finally that (4.31) may be written as:

$$C (w, X) = [c(w)X] X^{b-1} \tag{4.32}$$

where the term in square brackets is the cost function derived from a standard, constant-returns production function. Now observe that this is exactly the cost function obtained from the production function in (4.1), where the ith firm has a cost function $C^i(w, X_i) = [c(w) X_i] X^{-b}$, with total industry cost given by $C (w, X) = [c(w) X]^{-b}$. Thus it can be seen that the present formulation with endogenous numbers of specialized intermediate inputs is exactly equivalent to an external economies model with the individual production functions:

$$X^i = (X^a) F_i (V_i) \quad \text{where } a = (1-b) \text{ of } X = [\text{ sum } S^b]^{1/b}. \tag{4.33}$$

In other words, the "reduced form" of the complementary, specialized intermediate-inputs problem is the industry external economies problem. The analysis in the section on Multiple Equilibria is also applicable here.

Specialized, complementary intermediate inputs are one "micro-foundations" story behind the externality model. The lessons of the latter are quite applicable here. The market equilibrium is sub-optimal, with the X sector underproducing. Multiple equilibria may exist as in Figure 4.2. Gains from trade are not automatic, but are assured if the X sector expands with trade.

It may now be clear why the difference between national and international returns to scale (Ethier's term) was emphasized toward the end of the last section. If the specialized intermediate inputs are all non-traded, then the movement from autarky to free trade is as described in Figure 4.2. This may be called national returns to scale. Some producer services are non-traded, so that is a case in point. A second possibility arises from complementarities that result from close physical proximity (there are obviously many overlaps between these two catagories). Urban and regional economists call these agglomeration economies, and they form the basis of large cities. Indeed, the externalities model may then be more properly applied at the sub-national level.

The opposite extreme occurs when all the specialized intermediate inputs are (potentially) freely traded; these are referred to as international scale economies. The movement from autarky to free trade transforms both the external-economies and the intermediate-input functions to:

$$X_i = (X+X^*)^a F (V_i), \quad X = (nS_{ih}^b + n^* S^*_{jh}{}^b)^{1/b} \qquad (4.34)$$

where X^* is the foreign output of X, S_{ih} is the amount of the ith home intermediate used in the home country, and S^*_{jh} is the amount of the jth foreign intermediate used in the home country. n and n^* are the number of home and foreign intermediates respectively. The second equation implies the first if the countries have identical technologies, so that each good is produced in the same amount, regardless of country, and there is free trade. In this case, each domestic and foreign input uses the same amount and that amount is proportional to the share of the home-country's X output in total world output. For example, if each country is equally large and has an identical factor endowment so that each country produces the same amount of X, then in free trade each country will use half as much as each of twice as many intermediates. For example, if each country uses two units of each of ten inputs in autarky, they will use one unit each of twenty inputs in free trade.

Let n^a denote the number of intermediates produced in autarky in both countries and S denote their output level. Assume for the moment that these are constant. We then have:

$$X^f = (2n^a)^{1/b}(S/2) = (n^a)^{1/b} S (2^{1/b-1}) > (n^a)^{1/b}S \qquad (4.35)$$

Output increases in each country with the same resources allocated to the X sector. This is a "free lunch" in which output increases with no increase in inputs. If b = 0.8, for example, at constant inputs, output increases due to trade by $(2\exp(0.25))\, X^a = (1.19)\, X^a$ or 19 per cent. It is generally not an equilibrium to maintain the autarky level of n, so additional adjustments take place.

Figure 4.3 shows the movement from autarky to free trade, with the initial autarky production frontier shown as TT', and the initial autarky equilibrium at point A with price p^a. With two similar countries, the production frontier moves out to TT'' in free trade. Equilibrium production could be at a point like Q^1 and price ratio p^1. Consumption could take place above or below Q^1 on price ratio p^1 depending on the differences between countries.

I have extended Ethier's model in two other studies to examine gains from trade and the effects of protection (Markusen 1989, 1990b). As might be expected from Figure 4.3, the conditions for a country to be better off with free trade relative to autarky are much weaker than in the case of national scale economies. The condition for gains from trade is that trade expands the total (world) number of intermediates or division of labour relative to the division of labour in one country alone in autarky. It is therefore immaterial to the direction of real income gain whether or not the industry contracts in a given country. The benefits are captured from the increased division of labour and the implied capture of scale economies depending on total world output. As

Figure 4.3

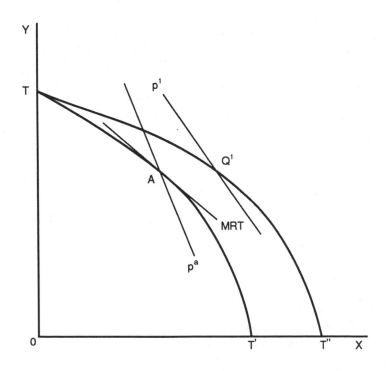

was the case with free entry and internal economies, gains are proportionally larger in a small country ($X < X^*$ or $n < n^*$ in equations 4.34). Productivity measures and real income indices should both respond positively to trade even though there is no change in domestic technology or domestic firm scale.

International returns to scale have related implications for protection. In most models with differentiated products, there is a small welfare gain to be captured by tariffs, which have the effect of distorting the terms of trade in the country's favour. With differentiated products, this is true even of small countries since their export products are, by definition, imperfect substitutes for foreign goods. Even small countries have local monopoly power.

With traded, complementary, intermediate inputs, this argument is much weaker. Foreign intermediates raise the marginal product of domestic factors at constant prices, and so tariffs that limit the import of such goods or services derationalize domestic production and even a small tariff may cause welfare to fall (Markusen 1990b). This can be seen in Figure 4.3. With national returns to scale, a tariff moves production around the production frontier. With international returns to scale, the tariff has the added effect of shifting the production frontier inward, such as from TT'' to TT'. It also follows that productivity will decrease in the X industry. Recall from the duopoly model that a tariff can increase productivity by expanding the output of the domestic firm (effectively national returns to scale) and in the free-entry model productivity might be unchanged if the industry expanded only through new entry. But with reference to (4.34), international returns to scale generally imply that a tariff cannot increase domestic output more than the loss of externalities from the foreign inputs. Real income can increase for a small tariff that improves the terms of trade more than the loss of productivity, but the latter must decrease.

To summarize, this section has presented a model that provides micro-foundations for the external-economies framework. It is a plausible model of the creation of specialized intermediate inputs (both goods and services) and it strongly emphasizes the importance of access to foreign specialized inputs for productivity, competitiveness and real income. Due to high fixed costs in R&D and other learning measures, a country the size of Canada cannot possibly hope to develop all the sophisticated intermediate goods and services by itself. This has specific implications for free trade in producer services, which generally have been more restricted than trade in final goods because the former impinge on immigration and foreign investment as noted earlier. These activities have been substantially liberalized under the US/Canada free-trade agreement.

Skilled Specialists, Training and Education

Many aspects of the role of public policy in training and education have long been debated. Most of these aspects are not of interest here. What is of interest is the much narrower question of the role in the economy of engineers, scientists and other skilled specialists.

A typical economist's response to the question of whether or not public policy should encourage the "production" (they are, after all, intermediate inputs) of more such workers revolves around externalities. Generally, these individuals do not capture privately all of the benefits of their training. If there are externalities, others capture some of the benefit, but there is then the further question of the form of the optimal policy. I shall comment on two issues — complementarities and capital market imperfections — the latter being much better understood.

There is some reason to suspect that the product-differentiation model described in the preceding section may be applicable to an analysis of scientists and engineers. It seems clear that such individuals accumulate specialized knowledge and individual expertise. There are surely cases where two engineers are perfect substitutes, but there are, perhaps, as many other cases where they are not. To put the matter differently, if a firm wishes to hire two engineers, is it better for both to be all-around generalists, or for each to specialize in a range of sub-specialties? If the answer is specialization, then there is an argument for using the specialized intermediate input model of the preceding section.

I believe there is a *prima facie* case for such specialization; I will show circumstances in which there is a market failure in the production of scientists and engineers, and then proceed to discuss appropriate policies. However, it must be remembered that here, as elsewhere in this study, the conclusions assume that the correct model is being used.

Suppose an individual can choose either to enter the work force as an ordinary laborer, denoted L, or to spend a period of time in training or obtaining an education, during which no income is earned. Skilled specialists are denoted S. Assume that all individuals have the same ability *ex ante*. Without outlining all the details of the model (which is a simplified version of Markusen, 1988), the production function in the "high tech" sector uses only skilled specialists. Assume further that each skilled specialist being created supplies exactly one unit of S. n denotes the endogenous number of skilled specialists.

$$X = [\ \mathrm{sum}(S^b) \ ]^{1/b} = n^{1/b} \qquad 1/b > 1 \qquad (4.36)$$

Assume that X producers are perfectly competitive and here, as in the previous section, it may be seen that there are increasing returns to the division of labour. Alternatively, the skilled specialists are complementary, with the degree of complementarity rising as b becomes smaller. Adding another bright young researcher to a group generally improves the productivity of the group as a whole. If the standard neoclassical model is correct, the marginal product of researchers must therefore fall as another researcher is added.

The key issue as to whether the optimal number of specialists is created depends on firm size and whether individual firms can internalize the complementarity. There are two definitions of marginal product for (4.36). The first is the change in X as a result of applying the time of an existing specialist for an additional hour, denoted MP_s. The second is the marginal product obtained by adding an hour of time obtained from an entirely new specialist to the firm, denoted MP_n. Let $c = (1/b - 1)$ (as in the previous section). At $S = 1$, these conditions are expressed as:

$$MP_s = dX / dS_i = (1/b) [\, sum(S^b) \,]^{1/b-1}(bS^{b-1}) = n^c \qquad (4.37)$$

$$MP_n = dX / dn = (1/b) [\, sum(S^b) \,]^{1/b-1}(S^b) = (1/b)n^c \qquad (4.38)$$

$$MP_n > MP_s = bMP_n \qquad (4.39)$$

It can be seen that adding an hour from a new skilled specialist is more productive than adding another hour from an existing specialist.

If the firms are sufficiently large to internalize the division of labour, then (4.38) is their perceived marginal product. But smaller firms that contract out for skilled specialists view the division of labour as fixed and (4.37) is their perceived marginal product. Assuming that the specialists are fully employed, however, the industry actually expands by creating more specialists and not by adding more hours to the existing ones. Equation (4.38) therefore represents the true or social marginal product of skilled specialists — which, in turn, exceeds the private marginal product. The market does not fully internalize the complementarities.

When firms cannot fully internalize the division of labour among skilled specialists, a market failure almost exactly like that of the previous section is created, but on a smaller scale. Figures 4.1 and 4.2 are appropriate to describe the situations when skilled specialists work only in one country and cannot serve foreign firms or migrate. The wedge between the price ratio and the marginal rate of transformation along the efficient production frontier is (again) given by $pb = MRT < p$. The gains from trade analysis can be carried out as in Figure 4.2. Real income and the productivity effects of free trade depend closely on whether or not trade results in an expansion of the high-tech sector.

The observed importance of management and engineering consulting firms, accounting, legal, financial, and marketing firms, suggests that this model is empirically relevant. Firms in the modern economy cannot fully internalize the division of labour (see McFetridge and Smith, 1989; Polese and Verreault, 1989; and Hammes, 1989 for recent studies). We thus have a *prima facie* case for intervention.

There are two important variations on this model that help to suggest appropriate policies. In one variation, skilled specialists such as consulting engineers can serve firms in both countries. (Some evidence on the quantitative importance of this is found in Polese and Verreault.) In the second variation, specialists can work only in one country, but they can migrate.

When the consulting engineers can serve firms in both countries, then the situation shown in Figure 4.3 exists. Free trade in consulting services leads to an increase in the world division of labour and the production frontiers of both countries shift outward. This is similar to the effect of a free improvement in technology arising from trade. The conditions ensuring gains from trade are easily satisfied, however, and the size of any gain is possibly significant. Foreign specialists are not perfect substitutes for domestic specialists and, indeed, the response of the larger market is for all engineers to become more specialized in a narrower range of skills and problem areas. The free trade equilibrium at Q^1 in Figure 4.3 is still not optimal and so there is some scope for policy to create more specialists. But part of any subsidy is captured by foreign firms, since each new specialist serves both countries.

This last point becomes more significant if the skilled specialists who work in one country can migrate. Suppose there is an initial equilibrium where specialists are indifferent to migrating. Assume, too, that the engineers are perfectly mobile, caring only about income and not about where (i.e. which country) they work. Now suppose that the Canadian government subsidizes the training of more engineers. This drives down the return to Canadian engineers and the market returns to equilibrium, with the new Canadian engineers emigrating to the United States or elsewhere. The beneficiaries of the policy are firms in the United States. The problem is exacerbated by high personal income tax rates in Canada.

Of course, engineers and others are unlikely to be perfectly mobile in this sense, but there is certainly evidence that the model is relevant. Canada has lost many specialists, including engineers, scientists and medical doctors to the United States and, conversely, has attracted many others from abroad, who were trained at their home-country's expense. The appropriate policy to deal with this type of market failure in an open economy is to focus on the use, and not on the creation, of scientists and engineers. If the output of these skilled workers is R&D, for example, then to subsidize R&D directly through grants and tax breaks is a better policy than to subsidize education and training. In an open economy, it is preferable to charge full cost for the education of skilled specialists and then subsidize their use rather than to subsidize their education and then tax their higher incomes when they enter the work force.

The problem with this theory is that it runs counter to other traditional arguments about support for higher education which include issues relating to capital market imperfections and uncertainty. It is argued that capital markets are sufficiently imperfect that students have difficulty borrowing anything against the collateral of their future human capital. Banks do not respond positively to this notion, partly because human capital cannot be attached upon default of a loan. Similarly, students may view specialized training as uncertain and risky, whereas society pools those uncorrelated risks across a large number of individuals, thus making the actual social or aggregate investment much less risky.

Superficially, this problem may appear to have nothing to do with the externality problem. Yet, insofar as capital market imperfections constitue a market failure, it is a market-failure argument. This point is discussed further in the section on R&D below. The externality argument suggests that subsidies be directed to the use of skilled specialists rather than to their creation, and this runs directly counter to the capital market argument. However, the capital market/uncertainty problem may be better understood, so perhaps more attention should be paid to the migration problem.

Finally, some comments on productivity. Measures of productivity and industry competitiveness certainly increase with the creation of more skilled specialists — provided they stay at home! More correctly, it can be said that productivity and competitiveness increase with the domestic use of skilled workers, wherever trained. However, such an increase in productivity can only be achieved at a cost, so it is therefore a cost benefit equation that must be examined. This point was made in Chapter 2, where it was noted that there is no special magic about increasing output through R&D or through capital accumulation. If the model of this section is roughly accurate there are, however, several market failure arguments that support channeling resources toward skilled engineers, managers, and so forth. Unfortunately, those arguments do not provide much help in determining the form of intervention.

Research and Development

Research and development is generally considered to be a good thing — at least until the bill arrives. It is recognized that R&D contributes to increased productivity, competitiveness, and real income, but there is, of course, a cost. The typical response of an economist to suggestions that R&D be encouraged is to question the need. If there are no distortions or externalities, then private decisions to commit resources to R&D rather than to other uses are optimal. A dollar invested in R&D yields the same payoff as a dollar invested in physical capital. Yet, empirical studies consistently indicate high private returns from R&D and point to a significant gap between private and social returns to R&D. Thus there does appear to be a *prima facie* case for investigating the issue further.

This section considers three possible reasons why the return from more R&D may be greater than the social opportunity cost of the funds. The first reason relates to issues of strategic competitiveness as discussed in Chapter 3;

the second relates to spillovers among firms, such that individual firms cannot appropriate all the returns to their R&D; and the third relates to risk and uncertainty.

Consider first a world where firms are imperfectly competitive and produce with increasing returns. It was demonstrated in Chapter 3 that if there is a Cournot competition in such a world, firms under-produce. In the case of the duopoly, it was seen that a subsidy to the domestic firms increases firm scale and gives them a larger share of world profits, therefore improving domestic welfare. Now, suppose that R&D helps reduce the marginal costs of domestic firms. It then follows from the same line of analysis that firms in Cournot equilibrium under-invest in R&D. A direct or indirect subsidy to R&D will stimulate investment in R&D, which lowers marginal costs, which increases equilibrium output, and which ultimately increases real income. Measures of productivity and competitiveness all move in the same direction. This line of argument was originally introduced by Spencer and Brander (1985) and it comes to the appealing conclusion that subsidized R&D support is a good thing.

There are serious problems with this line of argument, however, even if we accept the Cournot model and its conclusion that firms under-invest in R&D. The first problem is the free-entry argument that was developed in Chapter 3. The R&D subsidies create positive profits for those firms that already exist within the industry; the subsidies also create incentives for new firms to enter. · If entry is relatively easy, then the effect of the subsidies will be to increase the number of firms rather than to increase the output of existing firms. The subsidy is thus welfare-reducing. If subsidies are to be effective in a world of relatively free entry, then existing successful firms should be the targets to discourage this sort of rent-dissipating entry.

The second serious flaw in the Spencer-Brander argument is that (despite the appealing title of their article) there is nothing in the model to differentiate the subsidized factor, — labelled R&D — from any other factor. In their own model, it is as beneficial to subsidize physical capital, skilled labour, or even unskilled labour as it is to subsidize R&D. Subsidizing any factor stimulates the output of the domestic firms (barring entry) and thus has the desired effect discussed in Chapter 3. It is only better to subsidize R&D than physical capital if the social rate of return to R&D is in excess of the private rate of return. But that is an entirely different point. The strategic subsidy argument per se does not single out R&D.

Now consider the case in which firms cannot appropriate all of the returns to their R&D. This problem is similar to the knowledge-capital problem discussed in the multinationals section of the preceding chapter. Knowledge capital is often characterized as having a public-goods property, in that it can be jointly consumed by many users (the blueprint example) whereas a machine can only be used (consumed) by one user at a time. More to the point for present purposes, knowledge-capital is often only partly excludable, because it is often possible for one firm to gain access to another firm's knowledge capital. Many methods come to mind, from reverse-engineering to outright theft.

Suppose that X_i is the output of the ith firm in the X industry, and that it uses a vector of inputs V_i and invests in R&D, denoted as R_i. A simple static model makes the relevant point: assume that each firm in the X industry also receives a spillover effect of bR_j from an investment of R_j units of R&D by another firm j. Assume that b < 1, or that the R&D is not a pure public good among firms. The production function for the ith firm is given by:

$$X_i = F_i (V_i, R_i + sum (bR_j)), \quad j \neq i, \quad b < 1. \tag{4.40}$$

The private marginal product of R is expressed:

$$MP_r = dF_i / dR_i \tag{4.41}$$

The social marginal product of and additional unit of R&D by firm i summed over all of the firms is:

$$MP^*_r = dF_i / dR_i + b (n-1) dF_j / dR_i \tag{4.42}$$

Assume that all firms have the same production functions so that the subscript on F can be dropped. Then:

$$MP^*_r = [1 + b(n-1)] dF / dR_i \tag{4.43}$$

Comparing equations (4.41) and (4.43):

$$MP^*_r = [1 + b(n-1)] MP_r > MP_r \tag{4.44}$$

In equilibrium, the social marginal product of R&D exceeds the private marginal product. Suppose, for example, that there are 11 firms, and that the spillover factor is 10 per cent, b = 0.1. Then from (4.44), it can be seen that the social rate of return is exactly double the private rate of return. This example corresponds, generally, with the findings of Bernstein and Nadiri (1988).

In this type of situation, equilibria occur such as illustrated in Figures 4.1 and 4.2. The R&D-intensive X sector underproduces in market equilibrium and policies to stimulate R&D (or the R&D-intensive sector) are beneficial.

One qualification (which may now sound familiar) should be advanced. When the spillovers are international in scope, then the conditions described in Figure 4.3 apply. There are externalities among Canadian firms such that the price ratio is not tangent to the production frontier, but there are also positive externalities received from foreign R&D such that the production frontier moves out relative to its position in autarky. It is difficult to imagine spillovers occurring among Canadian firms but not between Canadian and American firms. Recognizing that this occurs in the real world, efforts to stimulate Canadian R&D necessarily result in benefits for U.S. firms. As in other examples in this chapter, the benefits from what is clearly a beneficial policy in a closed economy are partly dissipated as gains to foreigners. Conversely, Canada benefits from any pro-R&D policies adopted in the United States.

The final factor to be considered in the R&D equation is risk. A number of authors, such as Bernstein and Nadiri (1988) and Grilliches (1987), contend that even the private return to R&D is high relative to the private rate of return to physical capital. A possible explanation is that an investment in R&D is a much more risky undertaking than an investment in physical capital. The success of an R&D venture is highly speculative and has a very high variance. Firms are much more likely to know exactly what they are getting from purchases of plant and equipment. If firms are reluctant to take risks, this will drive the observed rate of return to R&D above the observed rate of return to physical capital, which is exactly what the studies show.

Suppose that a firm has a utility function $U(PR) = PR^{.7}$ where PR is profit. The utility function is concave with respect to profits, indicating that a dollar lost decreases firm utility by an amount that is greater than the amount of increased utility when a dollar is gained. Suppose that a firm can invest $1 million in an R&D project, with two possible outcomes (occasionally referred to as "states of nature"). One outcome is a success; the other is a failure. If the project is successful, the firm earns $3 million; if it fails, the firm loses the $1 million. Suppose each outcome occurs with probability 1/2. The expected return ER (in millions) from the project and the expected utility of the project can be expressed:

$$ER = (\$3)(1/2) + (\$0)(1/2) = \$1.5 \tag{4.45}$$

$$E(U) = (\$3)^{.7}(1/2) + (\$0)^{.7}(1/2) = 1.0788 \tag{4.46}$$

The expected return is a 50 per cent rate of return on its original investment. How should the expected utility be interpreted? What is the certainty-equivalent investment required by the project that yields the same amount of utility; that is, the investment that produces the same level of payoff irrespective of the outcome. This is expressed:

$$E(U) = (\$1.114)^{.7}(1/2) + (\$1.114)^{.7}(1/2) = 1.0788 \tag{4.47}$$

Thus, the risky R&D project that yields an expected return of 50 per cent is viewed in the same way as a completely safe investment that yields only 11.4 per cent. In such circumstances, a high average *ex post* rate of return on private R&D will be observed.

What is the relationship in this case between the private rate of return and the social rate of return? The literature on risk bearing suggests that much of this issue turns on the correlation among the risks of different projects. Suppose, as an extreme example, that there are two firms, each undertaking a R&D project, and each a mirror imagine of the other, in the sense that if the project undertaken by firm A fails then the project undertaken by firm B succeeds and vice versa. If both projects are then considered jointly for an investment of $2 million, a return of $3 million — or a 50 per cent rate of return — will be earned with certainty. When the symmetric projects have risks that are perfectly negatively correlated, there is no aggregate risk to society. Put another way, if the market cost of capital is 11.4 per cent, then the symmetric negatively correlated projects should be undertaken when the expected returns are only 11.4 per cent. If the social rate of return is 11.4 per cent, then the projects will be undertaken privately only when the rate of return is 50 per cent. This represents a very large gap between social and private rates of return. The assumption of perfect negative correlation of risks is the extreme case, and the gap between the social and private rates of return from the two projects goes to zero as the correlation between the returns goes from minus 1 to plus 1.

The counter to the argument that a gap exists between the private and social rates of return is that this is exactly what private capital markets are all about. Capital markets pool risks and if they do so with great efficiency, then high-risk projects are undertaken when they can be justified in terms of their social rate of return (assuming away spillovers here and focussing only on risk). Whether or not private capital markets in Canada pool risks efficiently is beyond the scope of this study. It is said that venture capital markets are poorly developed in Canada, but I have no proof of this.

The riskiness of private investment is partly cushioned by the tax system, which taxes successes and "subsidizes" losses (through write-offs). At modest tax rates, it is possible that this improves the attractiveness of risky projects. Suppose in the previous example that there is a 25 per cent tax rate on profits including a 25 per cent write-off provision on losses. In the "good" state of nature, a firm received $3 million, or $2 million profits above its $1 million investment, so it pays $500,000 in taxes on the profits for a net revenue of $2.5 million. Conversely, in the "bad" state of nature, the firm loses $1 million (profits are -$1 million) and consequently receives a credit of $250,000 against other tax liabilities for a net revenue of $250,000. The after-tax utility of the investment project is then expressed by:

$$E\,(U) = (2.5)^{.7}\,(1/2) + (0.25)^{.7}\,(1/2) = 1.139 \qquad (4.48)$$

The certainty-equivalent return is:

$$E\,(U) = (1.204)^{.7}\,(1/2) + (1.204)^{.7}\,(1/2) = 1.139 \qquad (4.49)$$

The certainty-equivalent rate of return is now 20.4 per cent. The firm will undertake the project if it can borrow at an interest rate lower than 20.4 per cent which is somewhat higher than the figure of 11.4 per cent in the absence of the tax. The tax system has the effect of raising returns in the bad state and lowering them in the good state, and in this example there is a net benefit to the firm. Of course, this is true only up to a certain tax rate, since it can be seen that as the tax rate goes to 100 per cent, the earnings of the firm go to $1 million in both states of nature, E (U) goes to 1, and the risky project has a certainty-equivalent of zero rate of return.

In summary, there are many reasons why Canada may be under investing in R&D. The three reasons discussed here, however, are the strategic motive of supporting Canadian firms in the international market place, the spillover problem which implies that firms cannot capture the full return on their investments and, finally, the argument relating to capital market failure. The weight of these arguments is, of course, a question for future empirical study, although measurement of high private rates of return to R&D and social rates of return that substantially exceed even these private rates does not suggest that there is a *prima facie* case for further investigation and for considering public policy support for R&D.

Dynamic Comparative Advantage

Research on dynamic or acquired comparative advantage is still in its infancy, but it is beginning to attract more attention from theorists. Important works include Krugman (1981), Romer (1986, 1988), and Lucas (1988). In the context of an open economy, important work has also been done by Grossman and Helpman (1988, 1989). To set out some of the key ideas, I again rely on an analytical framework developed by Ethier (1982). To some extent it also follows the issues described in Markusen (1990b). The basic idea is that certain processes are cumulative, and/or that certain changes to an economy are irreversible. Some conditions, whether "natural" or "man-made" (i.e., manipulated by policy) can have permanent consequences.

Assume that the final good, X, is, again, assembled from intermediate inputs according to the production function:

$$X = [\, \text{sum}(S^b) \,]^{1/b} \qquad 0 < b < 1. \tag{4.50}$$

The cost function for an individual input is:

$$C_i = M(w)S_i + F(w) \tag{4.51}$$

where w is a vector of factor prices. Assume that there is only one other good, Y, produced with constant returns to scale by a competitive industry.

Unlike earlier analyses using this model, assume that there are many time periods and that there is perfect foresight. Assume that F is incurred only once. F is therefore like non-depreciating knowledge capital. Once a firm acquires some specific knowledge, that knowledge does not depreciate and it can be passed on without cost to future workers (a chemical formula or a blueprint is a good example). Of course, such assets can depreciate in the economic sense if they have to compete against new and better products.

Assume that producers assess the present value of their profits when making an entry decision and, finally, that there are initially two absolutely identical countries. The production frontiers for the two identical countries/economies are shown in Figure 4.4 by TT'.

To understand the basic issues of dynamic comparative advantage, a simple assumption can be made. At the outset, (i.e., during the first period) through some unspecified "accident of history", firms in the home country can enter X industry, but firms in the foreign country cannot because they do not have access to the required technology, there are patent or other impediments, or whatever. The first-period equilibrium is then depicted as in Figure 4.4 where TT' represents the identical production frontiers (potential in the case of the foreign country) in the two countries. The home country produces at Q^0 and consumes at C^0, with the first-period price ratio given by p^0. The foreign country specializes in Y at T, and consumes at C^{*0}. The home country exports good X and the foreign country exports good Y. Both countries gain from trade (C^{*0} is on a higher indifference curve than that through T), but these are obviously very unevenly distributed.

Figure 4.4

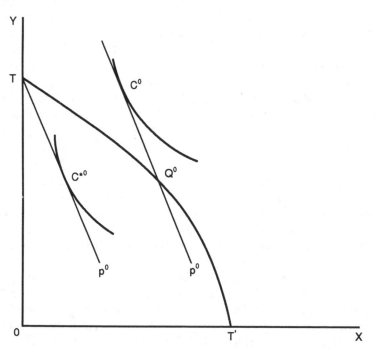

Assume that the foreign country can enter the X industry only during the second period. In the standard neoclassical model, even a dynamic model using depreciating physical capital, this initial difference due to the accident of history has no long-run consequences. The return to X sector capital (the fixed costs F) in the foreign country is higher and, as time passes, capital is also accumulated more quickly in the foreign country. The two countries approach the same level of steady-state consumption asymptotically. The initial advantage of the home country is dissipated in the long run.

The present model does not necessarily have the property that initial advantages are dissipated in the long run. Because knowledge capital is fully non-depreciating, the home country "inherits" a number of existing intermediate goods or "bits of knowledge capital" at the beginning of the second period. As noted earlier in Section 4, the specialized intermediate inputs are complementary, implying that the existing inputs at the beginning of the second period raise the productivity of additional new intermediates. Recall from (4.23) that the price of an intermediate, p_s, is expressed by the simple formula:

$$p_s = pn^c, \qquad c = 1/b - 1 > 0 \tag{4.52}$$

The price of an intermediate good, for a given price of X (p), is increasing as the number of intermediates increases. Another way to express the result is to say that there are dynamic increasing returns in the X sector.

At the beginning of the second period, the home country inherits a productivity advantage. It also draws more resources from the Y sector, however, and this raises the price(s) of the factors used intensively in the X sector. Thus, the overall competitive advantage of the home country at the beginning of the second period is not clear. What is clear is that at the beginning of the second period the production frontier of the home country has shifted, as shown in Figure 4.5, to TT'' while the frontier of the foreign country remains at TT' (assuming there is no primary factor accumulation). The fixed costs invested in the home country do not have to be reinvested in the second period, and so more X can be produced at the same level of Y production.

There is generally additional entry in the second and subsequent periods or, alternatively, all of the division of labour does not occur in the first period. The entry of additional firms not only drives factor prices higher as additional resources are drawn from the Y sector, but final consumption also falls, and impatient consumers thus bid up the returns to producing X relative to the present value of the returns from investing.

In an earlier paper (Markusen 1990c) I demonstrated the possibility of two alternative outcomes in the second period. First, it may be that the inherited productivity advantage of the home country is sufficiently strong that the foreign country cannot enter during the second period, even though it is "permitted" to do so. The productivity advantage of the home country is apparent because it can maintain a sufficiently low price for good X that the

Figure 4.5

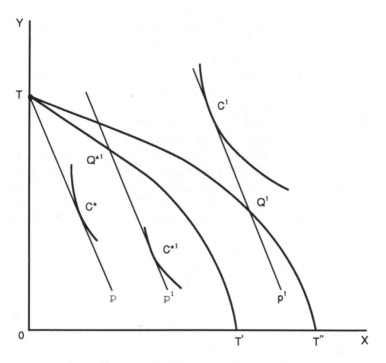

foreign country remains specialized in good Y. This is shown in Figure 4.5 with the foreign country producing at T and consuming at C^* with price ratio p^1. The home country produces at Q^1 and consumes at C^1.

The foreign country is generally better off than it was in the first period because the price of good X falls from its first period level (otherwise the foreign country could not be blocked from entering the industry during the second period). Consequently, the foreign country has a pure terms-of-trade gain. In relative terms, however, the foreign country tends to fall further behind due to the increased productivity in the home country. It is clear that the measured gap in output per worker must increase. Total factor productivity may or may not increase, depending on whether the accumulation of knowledge capital is included in the estimates of the capital stock or in the residual. In most studies, it is the latter.

The other equilibrium involves the foreign country entering, as shown in Figure 4.5 with production at Q^{*1} and consumption at C^{*1}. Although the home country is more productive, the enlarged X industry drives up the prices of the factors used intensively in that industry such that the foreign country can no longer be kept from entering the industry. Even in this case, however, I produced examples by simulation that had the foreign country falling farther behind in relative terms (Markusen, 1990c). This outcome is more likely because the first period is longer (it is defined by the length of time the foreign firm is barred from entering, not as one year) and the discount rate is lower. In other words, the more significant the head start of the home country, the more likely it is that the foreign country will fall further behind. So, even in this case where the foreign country can enter after the first period, there is still no neoclassical presumption that the late entrant will catch up with the first entrant. It may never catch up, it may have a permanently lower productivity in the X industry, and it may forever be an importer of the increasing returns good. Of course, the foreign country may still be able to improve its welfare over time as the price of X falls due to the capture of dynamic increasing returns, but its welfare will continue to lag behind what it could have been had it not suffered the initial disadvantage of late entry.

These results have interesting implications for public policy. The previous chapter dealt with internal scale economies and focussed on the ability of government to manipulate marginal price/output decisions to the country's benefit or detriment. Here, the focus is the possibility of manipulating the entire long-run structure of comparative advantage and trade by temporary policies.

The infant industry argument of the 1950s justified temporary policies to encourage the creation of specific industries, after which, it was argued, the policies could be removed. This argument was put down rather forcefully by trade economists of the CRS/PC school and it has all but disappeared (although it was included in a recent publication as a historical curiosity — am example of economists going wrong). The present model resurrects the possibility of such policies in a world of dynamic increasing returns. It is conceivable that some rather limited temporary policies can induce a number of domestic firms to enter some new industries and so kick the economy onto an entirely new path. (In an earlier paper, Markusen, 1990c, I suggested examples of such welfare-improving policies.) Equally conceivable, and perhaps more desirable, it may be of great benefit to a country if foreign entrants into a domestic industry can be blocked temporarily in order to give its domestic industry a head start. It is often suggested that Japan artificially generated its microprocessor (chip) industry in this manner. Because Japanese firms were not competitive with American firms the Japanese effectively closed their market to American firms, thus allowing their own firms to develop in a protected environment (Baldwin and Krugman, 1987). After sufficient time, however, Japanese firms became so competitive they were able to challenge American firms in their own home market.

Summary

This chapter draws together a number of seemingly unrelated issues involving externalities, R&D, education, and dynamic increasing returns. The basic unifying idea is the model of production externalities in a competitive economy. With such externalities market equilibria are, in general, not efficient; the price plane is not tangent to the production surface and there can be multiple equilibria, some of which are preferable to others. As in the case of internal returns to scale, there is consequently a role for public policy in stimulating the outputs of the relevant industries.

This model was applied in a number of different contexts. First, it was shown how the existence of complementary intermediate inputs or the productivity of increased division of labour, together with the existence of fixed costs, generates a market outcome that is essentially the same as that generated by the external economies model. The extent to which such inputs are freely traded is an important question in determining the gains from trade and the role of public policy. It was noted that in a small economy, access to a full range of specialized inputs, some of which may be impossible to develop at home, is vital insofar as the productivity and competitiveness of the home industry are concerned.

The same issues arose in the section on education, and the possibility was suggested that skilled specialists such as scientists and engineers may not be able to capture all of the gains in productivity they generate, and hence they are undersupplied in market equilibrium. Here, the crucial public policy issue is whether or not such individuals should be permitted to migrate freely. If they can, then public policy should focus on the use and not the creation of skilled workers.

Similar points were again made in the section on R&D. There it was argued that firms are not able to appropriate all of the returns from their investments and so R&D is undersupplied in market equilibrium. R&D-intensive sectors under produce in market equilibrium. As in the case of skilled workers and specialized intermediate inputs, an important factor for public policy is whether or not these R&D spillovers are international in scope. It they are, then policies to stimulate R&D partially benefit foreigners and, conversely, foreign policies partially benefit us. It is a moot point, however, as to how much to free-ride on foreign R&D.

The sections on education and R&D discuss the role of risk in undertaking investments. At first glance, these subjects may appear remote from the externality arguments, but the fact is that they tie in quite well. The standard view is that in a world of perfect capital markets there is no argument for market failure and policy intervention due to risk. But if capital markets are imperfect, then market failures do occur and there is therefore a role for policy. It may be that the lack of appropriate collateral contributes to capital market imperfection through borrowing to finance education and training, and that a lack of information and expertise also contribute to market failures in the capital market for R&D.

The final section develops a model similar to the one used to illustrate dynamic comparative advantage and dynamic gains from trade. This is a relatively new research topic but by using the monopolistic-competition model, researchers have constructed plausible cases where small initial differences between countries can be permanent — and indeed become magnified — in the long run. In the case developed here, there is a role for public policy to alter initial conditions, rather than to concentrate on marginal price/output decisions.

In all of these examples, market failures and underproduction in the key sectors show up in productivity and competitiveness indices. As in other cases cited, the resulting productivity, which is lower than optimal, has little or nothing to do with "technology". It has rather to do with the functioning of the economy.

In certain cases, such as in the discussion of trade in specialized intermediate inputs and trade in producer services, trade liberalization itself may result in sizable productivity gains that are quite different from or additional to the terms-of-trade effects that are the sole source of gains from trade in the CRS/PC model. With carefully constructed policies, the various externality arguments have no case against free trade.

Non-technical Summary

Introduction: Scope, Purpose and Central Concepts

This chapter is a review of the entire study and presents a non-technical summary of principal arguments and results. It is intended for a non-specialist reader and to stand alone; that is, it does not continually refer to points made in previous chapters.

I refer frequently to *Pulling Together* (henceforth *PT*), a statement published by the Economic Council of Canada, for which this study is a background report. My intention was to write this chapter so that it could be read independently of *PT*, but *PT* is nonetheless an excellent companion to this study — and, to my mind, an excellent document overall.

The purpose of this study is to analyze the determinants of, relationships among, and interpretations of four central concepts: 1) productivity, 2) trade performance, 3) real income, and 4) competitiveness. The study is essentially conceptual, and is also intended to provide an overall organizing and integrating framework for other more specific empirical studies. The analytical approach focusses on microeconomic issues, with some attempt to draw macro implications from the microeconomics. In a companion study, Richard Harris will no doubt contribute much of the macro-economic analysis that is important to the overall project, but which is missing here.

My hope is that this study will contribute to a better understanding of the determinants of indices of the four central concepts, and what a change in one implies about changes in the others. For example, what do changes in productivity or competitiveness imply about changes in real income? Is a deterioration in trade performance in one specific sector something to worry about? Does poor productivity performance in a sector necessarily mean poor technology and management, or might it simply be a reflection of Canada's factor endowment and small-scale due to its small market? Ideally, the study will help readers understand whether or not productivity and competitiveness are under the control of public policy, and which policies (e.g., domestic R&D policy versus trade policy) are most relevant and appropriate. In any prelude to policy analysis, we need to know what we should worry about, what we can influence, and what we should not worry about. For example, if Canada is observed to have a low and/or declining share of world trade in high-tech products, is this something to worry about, or is it merely the efficient outcome for Canada in a changing world?

The first task of this introduction is to address the problem of defining the four central concepts and considering the pitfalls, arbitrariness, and disagreements about those definitions.

Productivity

Productivity relates to the level of output that can be obtained from some given vector of inputs. Improvements in productivity are usually associated with underlying improvements in technology and organizational efficiency. There are many problems connected with data and the sophistication of alternative functional forms, but these are not important for the purposes of this discussion. Instead, my focus is on the interpretation of productivity indices.

Productivity is almost always measured (as opposed to defined) as a residual after all other easily identifiable and measurable quantities have been accounted for. This poses a central problem. Since it is a residual, a productivity change can be due to a very wide range of phenomena, including changes in the quality of the inputs or output, mismeasurement of the input or output levels, misspecification of the functional forms, and (especially) variations in scale and utilization of capacity.

A clear indication that productivity indices capture much more than technical and organizational change is that negative values are often calculated. Since it is difficult to believe in negative technical change, it is obvious that the effects of scale and capacity-utilization are not only included in the measure of productivity, they may sometimes dominate it.

A second qualification is that changes in productivity often carry a normative connotation that may or may not be justified. Is it "better" if real output increases because of an increase in productivity as opposed to an increase in the capital stock? If productivity increases are simply the effect of unmeasured increases in "knowledge capital" through investments in R&D, then this question cannot be answered without knowing the respective costs of the two types of investments.

Despite these considerations, it is clear that increases in productivity are closely related to increases in real wages in Canada. This is dramatically illustrated in Figure 6 of *PT* (p.6), which plots real wages against output per person-hour in Canada from 1946 to 1990. Because this is a measure of labour productivity, it mixes technical change and increases in capital — as well as other factors — per worker. Still, it is sufficeint to make the point that in the long run we earn what we produce.

PT also shows that Canada has fallen significantly behind other major industrialized countries in labour-productivity growth in manufacturing since 1980 (*PT*, Figure 13, p.20). Given the results in Figure 6 referred to earlier, this suggests slower real income growth in Canada.

Trade Performance

The concept of trade performance has to do with a country's exports versus its imports of goods and services and the changes in both over time. The term is used in a macro sense, as in measuring the current account balance, and in the micro sense of measuring the import/export shares of individual goods and services. In the latter case, shares and ratios can be calculated across goods within a country — as with the shares of all the different commodities included in total Canadian imports and exports. They can also be calculated for individual goods across countries, as with the share of Canadian exports of good X in relation to total world exports of X.

The difficulties with respect to the measurement of trade performance arise with the interpretation of the indices. The term "performance" has a normative connotation. Since the indices used are export shares (or export minus import shares) turning in a good performance has a decidedly merchantilist flavour. More specifically, an improved trade performance is not directly related to real income. Four examples help make this point.

First, trade performance in one sector can decline if the world population is growing faster than Canadian population such that Canadian exports in all sectors are falling relative to world totals.

Second, if that faster growth in the rest of the world is concentrated in resource-poor countries, then it is natural that they will move to specialize in manufacturing — including high-tech manufacturing and hence Canada's share(s) in non-resource-based industries may decline by more than the amount registered in resource-based manufacturing. In my opinion, the Economic Council of Canada worries excessively in *PT* about exactly these two changes (*PT*, pp.7-16).

Third, since shares must, by definition, sum to one, any change in the domestic economy will in general shift resources such that the share of some sector in total exports (imports) must fall (rise). If new natural resources are discovered in Canada, some labour and capital will be shifted out of the manufacturing sector such that the manufacturer's share of total exports (imports) will fall (rise). This should not be regarded as "bad", however, and the performance of the manufacturing sector should not be regarded as "poor".

Fourth, there is some danger in using the trade performance measures as indices of "revealed comparative advantage", as *PT* does in Table 2 (p.14). For example, it is possible for a country to export almost any good if the production of that good is sufficiently subsidized. Such exports do not reveal comparative advantage. If comparative advantage is defined as those goods that a country ought to export in order to maximize real income, then subsidized exports do not reveal comparative advantage. The statistics in *PT* Table 2 may therefore be "distorted" by government policy; in particular, it may be that Canada would be even more specialized in primary production and resource-based manufacturing without the cumulative effects of decades of the "National Policy".

In summary, the difficulties with trade performance measures lie in the interpretation and use of the measures, particularly in their normative interpretations.

Real Income

Most economists share a common conceptual view of what is meant by real income, but it remains difficult to measure. As with productivity, I prefer not to focus on measurement problems, but rather on how real income relates to the other central concepts. A principal point for purposes of this discussion is to draw a careful distinction between consumption and production. The two are closely linked in a closed economy, but the relationship is more complex and interesting in an open economy. The difficulty is that many writers (such as business journalists) focus on production measures instead of consumption measures.

At a number of points in this study I observe that the real income effects of some change and the trade performance (or production) measure of that change may have opposite signs. Real income in one year is maximized by maximizing imports and minimizing exports, since the latter are a giveaway to foreigners. But trade imbalances must be financed by the sale or purchase of assets and thus have implications for future consumption. However, the point is simply that the production/consumption distinction is crucial in understanding the link between trade performance and real income. Notwithstanding this last point, the long-run link between productivity and real income is dramatically illustrated by Figure 6 of *PT* as indicated earlier.

Competitiveness

Competitiveness is the most difficult and controversial of the four key concepts. There is little agreement on how to define it, how to measure it, or how to interpret the resulting indices, however measured. I have no simple definition to propose, and even if I did, I doubt that it would be productive to use a personal interpretation in this instance. My concern is with how the term "competitiveness" is used and I attempt to interpret those definitions in this study. In my view much of the difficulty can be traced to two sources. The first is the inappropriate use of the term in a normative sense in certain situations. Second, the term is often used in quite different senses on the micro and macro levels simultaneously. In short, the term "competitiveness" is often used simultaneously in contradictory senses.

Specifically, competitiveness is used in ways that relate closely to all of the other central concepts: productivity, trade performance, and real income. When a country is productive in the sense that it has a particular industry that is healthy and profitable, it is often referred to as being "competitive" even if it is small and/or import-competing in that country. In this case, "competitive" means productive and profitable. Even more often, however, competitiveness — and particularly changes in competitiveness — are associated with trade performance. If a country loses export share in a good, or import penetration increases, the county is described as "losing competitiveness" in that good. Current account deficits are sometimes interpreted as reflecting losses in competitiveness for the entire country. Thus, the United States was characterized as "losing competitiveness" throughout the 1980s.

Finally, competitiveness is sometimes equated with real income. Britain, for example, was deemed to be losing competitiveness in the 1960s and 1970s as its real income growth lagged behind the rest of Europe. The Far East is currently viewed as becoming more competitive, partly because of current-account surpluses, but also because real income growth rates are much higher in the Far East than elsewhere.

The difficulty has not only to do with the multiplicity of (often implicit) definitions, but also with the fact that they are often in conflict. As noted above, measures of trade balance for an industry or country may move in opposite directions in relation to measures of real income, and hence "competitiveness" based on one definition may produce results that are exactly opposite to those based on another definition. I suspect that much of the difficulty stems from the misuse of the term as a normative concept, and in the mixing of its micro and macro applications. I propose, therefore, that the way out of this difficulty is to keep a clear distinction between the use of the term in a strictly positive sense (as when referring to a declining industry "losing competitiveness") and its use in a normative sense (as when the X industry is described as "losing competitiveness and the implication of that description are desirable or undesirable — i.e. good or bad).

The macro/micro distinction is also important, and it is reasonable to suppose that macro uses of the term have valid normative content and can be readily agreed upon. A macro definition of competitiveness, focussing on real income in an open economy, is:

A country is competitive if it maintains a growth rate of real income equal to that of its trading partners in an environment of free and (long run) balanced trade.

This definition is close to that given in *PT*, except that *PT* does not refer to balanced trade. My definition raises at least two problems. First, there is nothing wrong with a current account deficit if it is the vehicle for financing real productive investment in a capital short country. Such a deficit could persist for years in a rapidly growing country. Second, there is clearly a catch-up phenomenon taking place around the world, with some countries in East Asia gaining rapidly, but starting from positions well behind those of the OECD countries. Assuming that imitation is much less costly than innovation, Canadians should not brand themselves as uncompetitive by comparing the domestic growth rate to those of countries engaged in this catch-up phase of development. This point is made in a half-hearted way in *PT*, (which, in my opinion, seems excessively preoccupied with Canada's declining share of world exports). From the work of John Dales three decades ago, we should understand the difference between maximizing the size of the Canadian economy and maximizing Canadian per capita income.

Along these lines, *PT* uses "competitiveness" in a macro sense to describe trade performance. In discussing Canada's shrinking share of world exports (it fails to note a falling share of world imports, as well), *PT* breaks this share into component parts —with the unexplained residual labeled "ability to compete" — in a totally arbitrary way. I urge readers of *PT* to use considerable caution in interpreting this measure this way. Consider, for example: a lower export level, all other things being equal, may just reflect a Canadian preference for current over future consumption relative to other countries; or it could reflect a larger non-tradables sector in Canada relative to newly industrialized countries.

Competitiveness is also used in several micro (industry- or firm-based) senses. There is nothing wrong with this, provided we understand what we are talking about and that we are careful about the normative connotations of the term. Even in micro terms, however, two definitions are possible. One focusses on productivity and compares total factor productivity, or unit costs of domestic firms to foreign rivals. The other focusses on trade performance, and tracks changes in export and import shares.

In some cases, the productivity/cost-based definition of micro competitiveness conflicts with the trade-performance-based definition, but in other cases the two can imply one another in a temporal sequence. For example, a technical improvement in an industry can give that industry a cost advantage in the short run, with little change in trade performance. In the longer run, additional firms enter the industry and output increases, implying factor-price changes, which in turn imply the dissipation of the industry's cost advantage in the long run. But, in time, the short-run cost advantage is transformed into a trade-performance improvement. Increased competitiveness in the sense of trade performance lags behind and, indeed, replaces increased competitiveness in the cost or productivity sense.

PT focusses on cost competitiveness: increases in productivity improve cost competitiveness; increased wages reduce it, and a rise in exchange rates reduces cost competitiveness even further. *PT* documents a strong and alarming increase in Canadian unit labor costs relative to the United States since 1986 (*PT*, Figure 15, p.28). Insofar as changes in cost competitiveness are "leading indicators" of changes in output and trade performance (as suggested in the previous paragraph), the changes in cost competitiveness documented by the Council in *PT* suggest that Canadian manufacturing has serious problems and, indeed, those problems have become increasingly apparent since 1988. It is important to note, as *PT* points out, that these problems clearly pre-date Canada-US free trade, and that the Free Trade Agreement cannot be held responsible for all of the present difficulties in the Canadian manufacturing sector.

Regardless of the choice of industry-based micro definition, there is always a caveat as to its normative significance. There is nothing "bad" about Canada losing competitiveness in low-wage, low-skill, labour-intensive manufacturing, although issues of adjustment costs and appropriate policies must, of course, be addressed. With this qualification in mind, I find the commonly-used micro definitions reasonably acceptable.

The next four sections of this chapter outline and summarize the four main analytical chapters of the study.

The Competitive Model

The traditional model used in international trade theory draws its paradigm from competitive general-equilibrium theory, and relies heavily on the twin assumptions of constant returns to scale (CRS) and perfect competition (PC) in production. In this world view, trade is generated by differences among countries. These differences are embodied in the Ricardian notion of comparative advantage: differences among countries imply that each is relatively better at producing some goods and services than others.

In the CRS/PC model, there are several possible underlying causes or bases for trade. The first is differences in production technology among countries. The second is differences in relative factor endowments among countries (absolute factor endowment do not determine the direction of trade with constant returns to scale, but they do help determine world prices and the volume of trade). A third difference is in preferences among countries, or alternatively non-homogeneous preferences such that a country's demands depend on per-capita income. A fourth difference is attributed to government distortions such as tax or subsidy policies.

The overwhelming amount of attention in trade theory in the CRS/PC tradition has been devoted to the first two of these, with factor endowments getting much more attention than differences in technology. However, much of the analysis and most of the implications relevant for our purposes are valid if any of the first three bases for trade characterize the world. Distortion-induced trade is something different; I will leave that for the moment and concentrate on the undistorted competitive model.

With technology, endowments, and tastes determining trade in an undistorted environment, several results are forthcoming. First, there are gains from trade whenever a country can trade at prices that differ from its autarky prices. The size of the gains from trade are proportional to the difference between world prices and the autarky prices.

Second, the direction of trade (which goods are imported and which are exported) is determined by the direction of the differences between the world and domestic autarky prices ratios. Countries reap gains from trade by selling to the world what they produce relatively cheaply and buying from the world what is relatively costly to produce at home.

Third, if world prices are fixed, free trade is optimal. There is no role for government to increase real income either by export promotion or by import restriction unless the country has some monopoly power in trade. In the latter case, small trade restrictions may be welfare-improving but export promotion is definitely welfare-reducing. Empirical studies suggest limited possibilities for an activist trade intervention policy for Canada — not to mention the obvious threat of retaliation.

Fourth, there is no normative significance to the direction of trade in the CRS/PC model. It is not "better" to export some goods than others. Whether goods exported are high-tech or low-tech is irrelevant to real income. World prices and competitive markets efficiently determine the direction of trade and specialization.

Fifth, there is no normative significance to "high value-added" sectors. Value added simply reflects the degree of intermediate input use, and intermediate inputs receive exactly their marginal product. Higher value-added sectors do not pay higher wages (for the same level of human capital) or higher returns to physical capital. The notion of encouraging high value-added sectors, therefore, is irrelevant in the competitive model.

Sixth, there is no normative significance to the level of output of an industry in the CRS/PC model. Output of an industry can only be stimulated by drawing scarce resources from other sectors, and the market correctly allocates those resources in the first place.

Seventh, there is no normative significance to one type of investment relative to another. Investments in R&D are not better in any sense than investments in physical capital, human capital, or resources. In the assumed absence of any distortions such as externalities, the market equates the marginal product of investment across investment types, and scarce savings are allocated efficiently.

Eighth, the existence of gains from trade do not depend on the economy's productivity level relative to its trading partners. Ricardo's important proof (now almost two hundred years old) shows that gains from trade can be captured by both of two countries even if one of them is absolutely better at everything. Gains from trade rely only on relative differences, or comparative advantage.

After making these general points, Chapter 2 addresses three specific determinants of trade, productivity, and real income. The first of these is factor endowments. By means of a simple model, we demonstrated that countries export goods using their abundant factors intensively. Thus, there is a clear and important link between factor endowments and the direction of trade. If Canada is well endowed with resources — broadly defined to include agriculture and forestry as well as mineral, coal, and petroleum — then Canada's pattern of specialization and trade will reflect this fact. Not only will these products be exported directly, but Canada should also export manufactured and semi-manufactured goods (fabricated materials) that use these inputs intensively. This is confirmed in *PT*, Table 2 (p.14), which clearly indicates a strong "revealed" comparative advantage in primary sector products and resource-based manufacturing. The burden of proof should clearly fall on those who maintain that there is something "wrong" with this pattern of specialization.

It is thus natural that Canada will have a smaller share of its exports or a larger share of its imports in industries unrelated to resources, including some high-tech products, relative to resource-poor countries. It is a flippant yet interesting point to note that Canada could improve its position in high-tech exports by throwing away some of its resource base. This illustrates the danger in concentrating on shares of goods in terms of exports and imports. Since shares must sum to one, the share of one good can only be increased at the expense of another. Major new resource discoveries in Canada would shift labour and capital out of manufacturing and the shares of those industries in exports (imports) would decline (increase). But there is certainly nothing "wrong" with the manufacturing sector in such a case. Biased increases in factor endowments will naturally have strongly biased output effects across industries and will include contraction in some sectors.

PT raises one legitimate point about specialization in primary products and resource-based manufacturing: prices of these goods may fall over time relative to other goods. *PT*'s Figure 5 (p.5) suggests that this has been the experience over the past 20 years, and to pick the early 1970s as a starting point clearly biases the issue. An examination of the same chart shows that prices of primary products are at much the same level they were relative to 1960-72 and energy prices are currently higher than for that period. If we take this longer view, there is no case for a secular fall in commodity prices. It can also be noted that the prices for electrical machinery and electrical consumer products have fallen dramatically over the last two decades; should we therefore avoid these "high-tech" industries?

Finally, the competitive model implies that the market is quite capable of reading and understanding price signals. If prices of our export goods fall over time, entrepreneurs and markets will choose optimal long-term adjustment strategies, gradually moving out of those industries — if that is, indeed, our best course.

It has already been noted that productivity is a residual measure. Thus if growth occurs primarily due to the growth of physical capital (including human capital) and to improvements in the resource base, then exercises in growth accounting will show increases in per capita income, but not increases in productivity (nor deteriorations of productivity in the contracting sectors). Again, there is nothing "wrong" with this, and there is nothing to suggest in the CRS/PC model that the country is under-investing in "intangibles" like R&D, relative to tangible and measurable inputs.

The second topic addressed in Chapter 2 has to do with changes in production technology. The source of such changes is not addressed. We draw merely on the implications of such changes for our four concepts. Technical change shifts resources into one sector, and therefore out of other sectors. The latter sectors will therefore register poorer trade performances, increased import penetration and/or losses of exports. There is a significant redistribution of income, with factors specific to expanding sectors being the big gainers, and factors specific to the contracting sectors being the big losers. A properly constructed index will identify the technical change as an improvement in productivity, and will not identify the contracting sectors as experiencing negative productivity growth. PT shows in Figure 3 (p. 3) that over the last three decades capital accumulation in Canada has exceeded the contribution of growth in total factor productivity. Somewhat disturbing in that Figure is the result that almost half the increase in real GDP per capita over the last three decades has been in the form of increased labour-force participation (e.g., working wives). This clearly has a limit and cannot continue to grow indefinitely.

Note that in the case of an increase in the endowment of a certain factor, and the case of a technical improvement in a certain sector, the contracting sectors can both be described as "losing competitiveness" if the definition based on trade performance is applied, but not if the definition based on productivity is applied. (Although, in the case of technical change, the contracting sectors are described as lagging behind "average" productivity changes.) In the short-run, both sectors could also be identified as uncompetitive if a cost definition, were applied, since the effect of the improvement in the other sectors is to drive up factor prices in the unaffected industries. But the movement of mobile factors out of the latter industries lowers the prices of specific factors in those sectors, and cost competitiveness is restored by the contraction of another industry. A short-run loss of competitiveness based on a cost definition becomes a long-run loss of competitiveness based on a trade-performance definition. A key point to emphasize, however, is that there is an increase in real income with the increased factor endowment or technical change. Thus, as was pointed out earlier, this is a clear case where the industry-based definitions of competitiveness do not have normative implications.

I turn now to the question of international price changes, and note that such price changes have similar effects in terms of competitiveness. A drop in price causes a sector to lose competitiveness in the short-run based on a cost or profitability definition, but a contraction of the industry re-establishes competitiveness, but this in turn deteriorates competitiveness measured by a trade-performance criterion. More importantly, the link between industry competitiveness, trade performance and real income cannot be determined without knowing the direction of trade which depends on preferences. Real income increases following a price change if, and only if, the relative prices of the export goods are rising relative to the prices of the imported goods. If world price increases for our imported goods cause our import-competing industries to be "more competitive", real income falls. This emphasizes an earlier point — it is very important in an open economy to maintain the distinction between production and consumption if the link between real income and the other three concepts is to be correctly understood.

A final point with respect to price changes is that they are a vehicle through which foreign productivity changes are transmitted to our economy. As Ricardo pointed out, trade is not like a war where one side necessarily gains and the other side loses. Unless foreign productivity increases are concentrated in their import-competing (our export) sectors, those productivity increases must result in a benefit through favourable terms-of-trade changes.

The next section of Chapter 2 discusses endogenous capital formation. The key point here is that any change in the economy (such a change in primary endowments, technology, or world prices) generally generates further changes in capital stocks. The direction of those changes generally reinforces the initial change and so responses to exogenous changes take time to emerge fully and are more elastic in the long run than in the short run. A technical improvement in one sector raises the return to capital in that sector, and generates long-run increases in the capital stock, thereby increasing the output of that sector more in the long run.

The final section of Chapter 2 addresses government policies. Here, the emphasis is on the difference between consumption and real income on the one hand and production and trade on the other. Two examples are discussed. The first involves export promotion. It is assumed that a government can fight to gain access to foreign markets or it can subsidize exports. In the example, the policies are set so that both have exactly the same effect on reallocating domestic production toward the export sector. Thus, industry or production-based measures of competitiveness and trade performance do not differentiate between the two choices. While admittedly ignoring the costs of negotiating market access, it is shown that, from the standpoint of real income, the two policies are radically different. The market access policy increases real income while the export subsidy reduces it.

The second policy involves an import tariff versus a voluntary export restraint. Here again, both policies are set to affect domestic production in exactly the same way, and so production-based measures respond to the policies as equivalent. However, they are very different in terms of consumption and therefore from a real-income point of view — with the VER being significantly worse.

The results of this section, along with those in the section on changes in the terms of trade, illustrate the difficult link between production and real income in an open economy. Measures of trade performance and industry-based definitions of competitiveness have, at best, no simple relationship to real income. These links must be clearly understood by policy analysts.

The Industrial Organization Model

There is a long tradition in Canada of analysis devoted to open-economy, industrial-organization, but until the 1980s it focussed exclusively on partial equilibrium and empirical cosiderations and was almost completely detached from international trade theory. During the last ten years, the two streams of literature (industrial organization and international trade) have become more integrated.

The fundamental modification to the competitive model is the introduction of scale economies or decreasing average costs in some industries. Competitive market structures generally cannot be supported with such technologies and so, theoretically and empirically, scale economies tend to be associated with imperfect competition. Imperfect competition in this context is a natural consequence of the technology and cannot simply be regulated away.

Several variables, especially firm scale or output level, that are of no positive or normative significance in the competitive model, now become important. Firm scale affects both measures of productivity and real income. Neither relationship occurs in the competitive model. The importance of firm scale in turn will imply quite different roles for and effects of public policy.

Chapter 3 develops a simple, one-factor, general-equilibrium model in which one sector produces a good with increasing returns to scale in a setting of imperfect competition. There is a fixed cost to beginning production, after which output can be produced at constant marginal cost. Thus, average cost always falls in relation to output.

There are five conceptually separate sources of gains from trade with increasing returns to scale and imperfect competition. The first is decreasing average cost. The large market supported by trade allows for each of the same number of products to be produced in longer production runs, and therefore at lower average costs.

Second, there may be a pro-competitive gain from trade in the more competitive trade environment. The technical argument is that trade increases the total number of firms in the market (with the number fixed in each country), and individual firms therefore perceive demand as more elastic (i.e., each firm perceives itself as having less influence over market prices). Firms find it individually optimal, therefore, to increase outputs, which generates a social welfare gain equivalent to the excess of price over marginal cost on incremental output.

Third, trade can rationalize the number of firms in each country at the same time as it increases the level of competition and the level of total output. For example, each of two identical countries may have five firms in a free-entry autarky equilibrium where no profits are earned. Trade leads firms to expand outputs, resulting in negative profits (losses) and the exit of some firms. If two firms exit in each country, the world is still left with six firms in total and more competition than in autarky. It is entirely consistent for the total outputs of the surviving firms to expand more than the losses due to exit so that both industry output and employment expand. This is, indeed, supported by the work of Baldwin and Gorecki and the counter-factual analysis of Harris and Cox.

Fourth, the gains from increased market size due to free trade can be captured in the form of more products at the same costs rather than in the form of the same products at lower costs. Although firm scale does not change in this case, scale economies are nonetheless responsible for the gains from trade since they limit the number of products in autarky in the first place.

Fifth, the same argument applies to specialized intermediate inputs. The larger market supports an increased division of labour, and Canadian firms have access to specialized machinery and consulting services that are prohibitively expensive to develop in a small domestic market.

I must emphasize that these are potential gains from trade and do not necessarily imply that countries capture them in practice. The next section therefore considers in a more rigorous way the criteria for actually capturing gains. Unfortunately it is possible to derive only sufficient conditions, and they are that gains are assured when trade results in a weighted expansion of the increasing returns firms. Increasing returns sectors are distorted by a gap between price (the value of an additional unit to consumers) and marginal costs (the cost of producing an additional unit), so expansion of an increasing returns sector generates a gain, and contraction generates a loss that must be added to, or subtracted from, the other sources of gains from trade. However, countries the size of Canada can hardly support large firms in all sectors, so the analysis goes on to show that expanding in some sectors and exiting entirely in others also generally leads to gains. There is no sin to exiting. Indeed, if there is a sin, it is in being small and inefficient in a sector.

The next section in Chapter 3 turns to a specific model, in which two countries each have one firm in the increasing returns sector and both firms engage in a Cournot duopoly (each firm can choose its own output, assuming that the output of the other firm is fixed). Here we show that when the country sizes and costs are roughly symmetric, free trade leads to expanded output by both firms in both countries. If the goods are very good substitutes, then it is possible that a firm might reduce its output if its country is much larger than the other country and/or it is at a significant cost disadvantage in production. In this case the sufficient condition for gains from trade fails, and the country could be worse off with trade. If this simple model is any guide, however, the cost differential has to be large and Canada is hardly the large country relative to its trading partners. There is nothing in the model to suggest that Canada is in a fragile position.

Section 6 conducts the same analysis with conditions of free entry and exit of firms in response to profits and losses. Empirically, this seems to be the relevant assumption. However, in this case we show an even stronger result that a country gains, even if it is larger and/or a high cost producer, although in the latter case it may be forced out of the industry.

Contrary to the results obtained from the competitive model, here there are more direct links among productivity, trade performance, competitiveness and real income. Firm output levels (in increasing returns sectors) are of direct significance for real income and for productivity measures. Measures of labour and of total factor productivity increase with firm scale as average costs fall (indeed, total factor productivity is more or less the inverse of average cost at constant factor prices and technology). Trade performance may or may not have any direct impact on real income, depending on how closely related it is to firm scale. If exports increase or import penetration decreases due to the entry of new firms at the old scale, there is no gain in productivity or real income. I emphasize in Chapter 3 that it is firm scale, not industry scale, that is the crucial variable. The micro (industry) definition of competitiveness based on productivity and cost is, therefore, a more reliable normative indicator than a definition of competitiveness based on trade performance.

Bearing these results in mind, the next section of Chapter 3 deals with trade policy. As in the previous chapter, there is no attempt to provide a comprehensive survey. Rather, the focus is on one policy, in order to develop the broad intuition that is applicable to many policy experiments. The policy chosen for analysis is a production subsidy to the increasing returns sector, a policy that can never be welfare-improving in a competitive, constant returns model. In the duopoly model, the effect of a small subsidy is welfare-improving for the home country and welfare-reducing for the foreign country. The subsidy also stimulates output from the firm with increasing returns in the home country, thereby allowing the home country to capture the gain of price minus marginal cost on the incremental output. The foreign firm reduces output and the foreign country suffers a welfare loss. This result is for trade that is initially balanced. As the subsidy becomes larger and larger, the deterioration of the terms-or-trade for the home country eventually make it worse off and the foreign country better off. Measured total factor productivity increases in the home country and decreases in the foreign country, and both the productivity and trade performance measures correctly track real income for a small subsidy (they certainly do not do so for a subsidy on a competitive sector).

Free entry has exactly the opposite result. The subsidy creates positive profits, which encourages the entry of new firms, and equilibrium is eventually re-established with more firms at the old scale of production. In this case, there is no positive firm-scale effect, no increase in measured total factor productivity, and a fall in real income. The foreign country is made better off because of a terms-of-trade gain, even if it is driven out of the industry. In this case, a definition of industry competitiveness based on factor productivity is, again, a more reliable guide to real income than a definition based on trade performance. Once again, industry scale is not a good guide to real income.

PT, unfortunately, has little to say about industrial-organization variables. There is some discussion of capacity utilization in Table 5 (p.22) and Figure 14 (p.24) as a factor in the productivity slowdown of the post-1973 period, but there is little else. One important point might be suggested. Trade liberalization in the Canadian economy during the post-war years may have been a significant contributor to the strong productivity growth documented in *PT* (Figures 3 and 6). It may also be a coincidence that productivity growth has slowed as the pace of trade liberalization has slowed. As noted above, firm scale expansion (or exit) as a consequence of trade liberalization will appear as a measured increase in total factor productivity. Similarly, the combined effects of various types of deregulation during this same time period may have contributed to the measured productivity increase via industrial-organization effects, although some of the important aspects of deregulation (such as those relating to foreign investment) occur well into the years marked by "productivity slowdown" (post-1973).

Research & Development, Education, Externalities, and Dynamic Comparative Advantage

Chapter 4 is devoted to a number of topics which, at first glance, may appear to be quite disparate but, for the issues at hand, are in fact rather closely related. A principal unifying theme is the existence of externalities broadly defined, and the inefficiency of market equilibria. As with the industrial-organization model, trade and policies to promote or retard trade will have added effects, depending on whether or not they expand or contract distorted sectors. In some cases there are direct connections between productivity and competitiveness measures and real income. Yet it is important to understand the true nature of the problem in designing public policy. In an open economy it is important to make careful distinctions between domestic and trade policies, and policies focussing on production versus consumption.

The next section develops a simple, general model of a positive production externality, which is then applied in several concrete situations in subsequent sections. It is shown that the price plane is not tangent to the production frontier, and the production set is non-convex. The first implies that market equilibria are not optimal; the second implies that there may be multiple equilibria, characterized by quite different welfare levels. As in the previous chapter, it is shown that trade generates additional welfare effects corresponding to the expansion or contraction of the distorted sectors. An expansion is a sufficient, but not necessary, condition for gains from trade.

This model is first applied to the analysis of complementary, specialized intermediate inputs, such as specialized machinery or consulting services. Increasing "division of labour" is productive, but is limited by the fixed costs of creating new specialized inputs. Market equilibrium in the model is characterized by a less than optimal division of labour. When a new firm enters, it confers a positive externality upon other firms, but it cannot capture the returns from doing so. Thus the sector under-produces in market equilibrium, a situation very much like that shown for the general externalities model, and the analysis of gains from trade proceeds accordingly. Productivity measures and real income are directly linked to the size of the sector. Neither relationship occurs in the case of the CRS/PC model, however.

One important question with respect to this model is whether or not the intermediates are traded. If so, then the externalities are international in scope. The benefits of trade are substantially larger and the conditions for gains from trade are substantially weaker. Free trade in such sectors is important to ensure that Canadian firms have the opportunity to capture efficiency and productivity gains from specialized inputs and services developed elsewhere since the

Canadian market is too small by itself to support a full range of such activities. Examples of such producer services include management and engineering consulting, finance, insurance, and marketing. Trade in these areas has been substantially liberalized under the US/Canada Free Trade Agreement.

In line with an earlier suggestion, this may be important in interpreting the productivity growth shown in Figures 3 and 6 of *PT*. Canada cannot produce a full range of intermediates, nor can it support a full complement of specialized consultants, engineers and managers. Trade liberalization since 1960 has provided Canadian firms with access to specialized foreign intermediate inputs, and has, thereby, increased the total factor productivity of Canadian firms.

The next section deals with questions related to training and education. There are, of course, many issues in this category but my focus here is on three questions: whether or not market outcomes are efficient; what are the possible sources of inefficiency; and what are the appropriate policy responses? The model developed in the preceding section was adapted to accommodate the problem of individuals acquiring specialized skills — which are imperfect substitutes for, or complements to, the skills of others. Thus, the section focusses more on engineers and managers than on skilled production workers.

Here again, it is shown that market outcomes may be inefficient when skilled specialists cannot capture the full benefits that they confer on other workers and firms. In such cases, the sector under-produces, and measures to stimulate its output are justified. But two important questions need to be answered. First, are the externalities international or strictly national in scope? Consulting engineers, for example, can work in the United States or Canada, or anywhere else, for that matter. So, any support for the training of such people partly confers benefits on foreigners and, conversely, foreign support for technical training confers benefits on us. Second, when such individuals decide to move to another country (after having been trained and employed in only one country) do they migrate in response to earning differentials? If so, then subsidies to technical education may result simply in emigration of highly-trained workers and the subsidy therefore benefits foreigners. In both of these situations, it is better to direct policy to support the use of skilled specialists in the economy rather than to support their training and education.

These ideas relate to pages 38 through 42 of *PT*, where the adoption of advanced manufacturing technologies and human and organizational factors are discussed. Clearly, technology is not simply a matter of buying a piece of equipment and turning on the switch. Technology has to be created, evaluated, implemented and accommodated to the use and needs of the skilled specialists who employ it. This is also made clear in Table 10 (p.35) of *PT*, which indicates that the majority of innovation costs in manufacturing are incurred after the research and design phase. Manpower and training policies must recognize this fact. The Council also notes that we are now in an integrated North

American (and to a lessor extent world) market for skilled workers and consultants. This places constraints on both federal and provincial governments with respect to levels of income tax etc. that must be recognized if governments expect to attract and retain the right specialists.

The claim that this is ongoing market failure in upper-level education argues strongly for the direct support of education and training. This claim is a capital-market failure argument to the effect that it is difficult and risky to borrow for higher education. Future human capital cannot be used as collateral, and individuals have risks of failure that are pooled for society as a whole such that there is no aggregate risk. These arguments are difficlut to evaluate, but if they do hold up empirically, then they suggest policies aimed at support for education rather than at end use.

The two sets of issues pull in different directions, but in both cases the sector using skilled specialists intensively under produces in market equilibrium, and measures of productivity, competitiveness, and real income all tend to move together. Measures of productivity and competitiveness accurately reflect real income.

The next section in Chapter 4 concerns research and development. Again, the focus I adopt is deliberately narrow. In a world with no externalities or other distortions, markets make efficient decisions on R&D just as they do with respect to other investments. Funds are correctly and optimally allocated among investments in R&D, physical capital, and human capital. There is no particular role for policy and there is no reason to be concerned about the allocation of funds to R&D. This section therefore considers several market-failure arguments and relates them to the general externalities model.

The first argument relates to spillovers. It is often argued, both theoretically and empirically, that firms cannot appropriate all of the benefits that accrue from the creation of knowledge capital. Innovations can be easily copied or imitated, and because knowledge capital often has the same "public-good" property as was discussed earlier in connection with multinationals. Limited empirical evidence supports this claim. In such a situation, R&D is under-provided in market equilibrium, and R&D-intensive sectors under-produce. Policies to stimulate such sectors are therefore justified because, again, there is a direct connection between productivity, competitiveness, and real income.

There is also the issue of whether or not spillovers are strictly national or international in scope. I find it difficult to imagine that spillovers are not international. In light of this, it should be remembered that Canadian support for R&D partialy benefits producers elsewhere and, conversely, foreign support for R&D partialy benefits Canadian firms.

A second argument has to do with strategic support for Canadian firms for the same reasons noted in the industrial-organization chapter. When there are increasing returns and imperfect competition in some industries, those industries may under-produce in market equilibrium. Measures to stimulate output increase productivity, competitiveness, and real income. Support for R&D is one such measure to increase the competitiveness and market share(s) of the domestic firms.

There are two very important caveats to this argument, however. First, if R&D subsidies simply attract new entrants and the industry expands only by new entry, then the policy is a failure. Firm-level output and not industry output is the key variable; competitiveness measured by trade performance (industry size) does not generally give the correct welfare signal. Second, the strategic argument itself does not suggest that support for R&D is better than any other method of encouraging industry expansion, such as training subsidies for skilled workers.

The third argument relates to risk and possible capital market failures. R&D projects may be risky for an individual firm, but if those risks are negatively correlated across all firms with R&D projects, then society bears less aggregate risk but R&D investment may also be less than the socially optimal amount. The counter-argument is that this is exactly what capital markets are for. Investors pool risks with diversified portfolios such that the market does create the optimal amount of R&D. Whether or not private capital markets in Canada optimally pool risks is an empirical question. It may be that capital markets do not have access to, and/or do not have the ability or expertise to evaluate, the information necessary to make the most efficient decisions in this connection.

PT documents a lower level of expenditures on R&D by Canada as a percentage of GDP relative to other major industrialized countries (Table 11, p.35, Figure 16, p.36). By themselves, these figures do not make a convincing case. Presumably, there is some natural pattern of comparative advantage in R&D (which is, after all, only another intermediate input) just as there is with respect to other goods and services. In line with the previous few paragraphs, however, the very high rates of return from R&D that have been documented suggest that these issues should be investigated further. These issues are not discussed in the detail they deserve in *PT* (see the short section on p.42), although they have been thoroughly researched by Pierre Mohnen in another background study for *PT*. The very high returns (private and especially social) estimated by Mohnen give a *prima facie* case for intervention of some sort in the R&D process.

The final section of Chapter 4 deals with dynamic comparative advantage, which is a relatively new area of research. The basic idea is that certain economic processes are cumulative, and/or that certain changes to an economy are irreversible. Initial conditions, whether natural or man-made (including by public policy), can have permanent consequences. I developed a simple model, based on the creation of specialized intermediate inputs, that follows as a natural extension of earlier analysis. Firms invest in learning and the output of the investment is non-depreciating knowledge capital that is complementary to other inputs. In this model, a country that gets a head start in the relevant industry inherits a productivity advantage (at the beginning of the next period) an advantage that may grow over time. It is possible, therefore, that two countries may get onto divergent growth paths as a consequence of some relatively small initial difference. This is very different from traditional models with constant returns and perfect competition where the consequences of diminishing marginal products are that countries eventaully reach a common steady state, independent of initial conditions; that is, initial differences disappear.

At present, little is known about the empirical relevance of this class of models and ideas. At a general level, industrialized countries are relatively similar and have become even more so over time. Yet, individual industries can also be identified where a country has maintained a permanent advantage after an initial head start. Cases can also be identified where trade barriers or subsidies were important in creating an industry which would not have happened otherwise (semi-conductors in Japan, wide-bodied commercial aircraft in Europe, for example). In a world of dynamic increasing returns, policy considerations must be expanded to include not only the manipulation of marginal price/output decisions, but structural issues underpinning the existence of an entire industry. This does not, of course, imply that we should embark on a program of manipulating our industrial structure. If anything, these dynamic scale economies emphasize the need for caution: today's policy decisions can have cumulative consequences by diverting the economy on to another development path that diverges from the original path. Enlightened policy picks the right path.

Bibliography

BALDWIN, John R. and Paul K. Gorecki, "The Relationship between Trade and Tariff Patterns and the Efficiency of the Canadian Manufacturing Sector in the 1970s: A Summary," in *Canada - United States Free Trade*, Volume II of the *Report* of the Royal Commission on the Economic Union and Development Prospects for Canada, ed. John Whalley with Roderick Hill (Ottawa: , 1985), pp. 179-92.

_____, "The contribution of the competitive process to productivity growth: The role of firm and plant turnover," Discussion Paper No. 769, Institute for Economic Research, Kingston: Queen's University, January 1990.

BALDWIN, J. R., Paul K. Gorecki and J. McVey, "Imports, secondary output, price-cost margins and measures of concentration: Evidence for Canada, 1979," Discussion Paper No. 263, Ottawa: Economic Council of Canada, 1984.

BALDWIN, J. R., et al, "The determinants of entry and exit to Canadian manufacturing industries," Discussion Paper No. 225, Ottawa: Economic Council of Canada, 1983a.

BALDWIN, J. R., et al, "Trade, tariffs, product diversity and length of production run in Canadian manufacturing industries 1970-1979," Discussion Paper No. 247, Ottawa: Economic Council of Canada, 1983b.

_____, Trade, tariffs, and relative plant scale in Canadian manufacturing industries: 1970-1979," Discussion Paper No. 232, Ottawa: Economic Council of Canada, 1983c.

_____, The relationship between plant scale and product diversity in Canadian manufacturing industries," Discussion Paper No. 237, Ottawa: Economic Council of Canada, 1983d.

BALDWIN, Richard, "Sunk-cost Hysteresis," National Bureau of Economic Research Working Paper No. 2911, March 1989.

BALDWIN, Richard and Harry Flam, "Strategic trade policies in the market for 30-40 seat commuter aircraft," *Weltwirtschaftliches Archiv* 125:3 (1989):484-500.

BALDWIN, Richard E. and Paul Krugman, "Market access and international competition: A simulation study of 16K random access memories," Ch. 7 in *Empirical Methods for International Trade*, ed. Robert C. Feenstra (Cambridge: MIT Press, 1988), pp. 171-97.

_____, "Persistent trade effects of large exchange rate shocks," *Quarterly Journal of Economics* 104 (November 1989):635-54.

BALDWIN, Richard and Richard Lyons, "Exchange rate hysteresis: The real effects of large vs. small policy misalignments," National Bureau of Economic Research Working Paper No. 2828, January 1989.

BEAUDREAU, Bernard C., "A strategic model of multinational firm learning," University of Western Ontario Ph.D. thesis, London, 1986.

_____, "Entrepreneurial ability, international trade and foreign direct investment:, *International Economic Journal* 3 (Autumn 1989):1-22.

BERNSTEIN, Jeffrey I. and M. Ishaq Nadiri, "Interindustry R&D spillovers, rates of return, and production in high-tech industries," *AEA Papers and Proceedings* 78:2 (May 1988):429-34.

BLOMSTRÖM, Magnus, et al, "What do rich countries trade with each other? R&D and the composition of U.S and Swedish trade," National Bureau of Economic Research Working Paper No. 3140, October 1989.

BLOMSTRÖM, Magnus and Edward N. Wolff, "Multinational corporations and productivity convergence in Mexico," National Bureau of Economic Research Working Paper No. 3141, October 1989.

BOVENBERG, A. Lans and Lawrence H. Goulder, "Promoting investment under international capital mobility: an intertemporal general equilibrium analysis," National Bureau of Economic Research Working Paper No. 3139, October 1989.

BOWEN, Harry P., et al, "Multicountry, multifactor test of the factor abundance theory," *American Economic Review* 77 (1986):791-809.

BRECHER, Richard A. and Ehsan U. Choudhri, "The factor content of consumption in Canada and the United States: A two-country test of the Heckscher-Ohlin-Vanek model," Ch. 1 in *Empirical Methods for International Trade*, ed. Robert C. Feenstra (Cambridge: MIT Press, 1988).

BROWN, Drusilla K., "Market structure, the exchange rate, and pricing behavior by firms: some evidence from computable general equilibrium trade models," *Weltwirtschaftliches Archiv* 125 (1985) 441-63.

BROWN, Drusilla K. and David M. Garman, "A review of the role of labor in recent international trade models," Seminar Discussion Paper No. 252, Tufts University, August 1989.

CABALLERO, Ricardo J. and Richard K. Lyons, "The role of external economies in U.S. manufacturing," National Bureau of Economic Research Working Paper No. 3033, July 1989.

CANADIAN LABOUR MARKET AND PRODUCTIVITY CENTRE, "Productivity and competitiveness," Ch. 3 in *Quarterly Labour Market & Productivity Review* (Winter 1989):16-20.

_____, "Feature Article - the linkages between education and training and Canada's economic performance," Ch. 4 in *Quarterly Labour Market & Productivity Review* (Winter 1989):21-31.

CAS, Alexandra, et al, "Productivity growth and changes in the terms of trade in Canada", in *Empirical Methods for International Economics,* ed. Robert Feenstra (Cambridge: MIT Press, 1988), pp. 279-94.

CAVES, Richard E., *Multinational Enterprise and Economic Analysis* (Cambridge: Cambridge University Press, 1982).

_____, Adjustment to International Competition (Ottawa: Supply and Services Canada for the Economic Council of Canada, 1990).

COCKBURN, Iain and Zvi Griliches, "Industry effects and appropriability measures in the stock market's valuation of R&D and patents," *AEA Papers and Proceedings* 78:2 (May 1988):419-23.

COHEN, Wesley M. and Daniel A. Levinthal, "Innovation and learning: the two faces of R&D," *The Economic Journal* 99 (September 1989):569-96.

DENNY, Michael, "A survey of research on Canadian productivity and competitiveness," mimeo, January 6, 1990.

DENNY, Michael and Melvyn Fuss, *Productivity: A Selective Survey of Recent Developments and the Canadian Experience*, Discussion Paper Series (Toronto: Ontario Economic Council, 1982).

DENNY, M., et al, "A report on productivity in the service sectors of Canada, Japan and the United States," mimeo, October 22, 1989.

_____, "Report on the comparison of manufacturing productivity in Canada, Japan and the United States," mimeo, January 18, 1990.

DIEWERT, W. Erwin, and Catherine J. Morrison, "Adjusting output and productivity indexes for changes in the terms of trade", *Economic Journal* 96, (1986):659-79.

DIXIT, Avinash, "Optimal trade and industrial policies for the U.S. automobile industry," Ch. 6 in *Empirical Methods for International Trade*, ed. Robert C. Feenstra (Cambridge: MIT Press, 1988), pp. 141-65.

DIXIT, A. K. and A. S. Kyle, "The use of protection and subsidies for entry promotion and deterrence," *American Economic Review* 75 (1985):139-52.

DIXIT, A. K. and G. M. Grossman, "Targeted export promotion with several oligopolistic industries," *Journal of International Economics* 21, (1984):233-50.

DOLLAR, David, "Employment and income effects of multinational production by U.S. computer firms," *International Economic Journal* 3 (Winter 1989):1-17.

DOLLAR, David, et al, "The factor-price equalization model and industry labor productivity: an empirical test across countries," Ch. 2 in *Empirical Methods for International Trade*, ed. Robert C. Feenstra (Cambridge: MIT Press, 1988), pp. 23-47.

DORNBUSCH, Rudiger, "Real exchange rates and macroeconomics: A selective survey," *Scandinavian Journal of Economics* 91 (1989):401-32.

EASTMAN, Harry C. and Stefan Stykolt, *The Tariff and Competition in Canada*, (Toronto: Macmillan, 1967).

EATON, J. and G. M. Grossman, "Optimal trade and industrial policy under oligopoly," *Quarterly Journal of Economics* 101 (1985):383-406.

ECONOMIC COUNCIL OF CANADA, "Project scope and methodology," Trade Advisory Committee Meeting, Competitive and Trade Performance Group, April 6, 1990.

_____, *Pulling Together: Productivity, Innovation, and Trade*, (Ottawa: Ministry of Supply and Services Canada, 1992).

EDWARDS, Sebastian, "Openness, outward orientation, trade liberalization and economic performance in developing countries," National Bureau of Economic Research Working Paper No. 2908, March 1989.

EMPEY, William F., "Contracting out of services by manufacturing industries," Discussion Paper, Institute for Research on Public Policy, May 1988.

ETHIER, W. "National and international returns to scale in the modern theory of international trade," *American Economic Review* 72, (1982):389-405.

FEENSTRA, Robert C., Trade Policies for International Competitiveness, National Bureau of Economic Research Conference Report (Chicago: University of Chicago Press, 1989).

FEENSTRA, Robert C. and James R. Markusen, "Accounting for growth with new inputs: A monopolistic-competition approach," University of Western Ontario working paper, 1990.

FELDSTEIN, Martin and Phillipe Bacchetta, "National saving and international investment," National Bureau of Economic Research Working Paper No. 3164, November 1989.

FRAUMENI, Barbara M. and Dale W. Jorgenson, "The role of capital in U.S. economic growth, 1948-1979," in *Measurement Issues and Behavior of Productivity Variables*, ed. Ali Dogramaci (Boston: Kluwer Nijhoff Publishing, 1986), pp. 161-244.

FRANKEL, Jeffrey A., "Quantifying international capital mobility in the 1980s," National Bureau of Economic Research Working Paper No. 2856, February 1989.

GOLDBERG, Linda, "Nominal exchange rate patterns: Correlations with entry, exit and investment in U.S. industry," National Bureau of Economic Research Working Paper No. 3249, January, 1990.

GOULDER, Lawrence H. and Barry Eichengreen, "Savings promotion, investment promotion, and international competitiveness," in *Trade Policies for*

International Competitiveness, ed. Robert C. Feenstra (Chicago: The University of Chicago Press, 1989), pp. 5-44.

GRILICHES, Zvi, "R&D and productivity: Measurement issues and econometric results," *Science* 237 (July 1987):31-5.

GROSSMAN, Gene M., "Explaining Japan's innovation and trade: A model of quality competition and dynamic comparative advantage," National Bureau of Economic Research Working Paper No. 3194, 1989.

GROSSMAN, Gene M. and Elhanan Helpman, "Comparative advantage and long-run growth," working paper, 1988.

_____, "Endogenous product cycles," working paper, 1989.

HAMMES, David L., *Shaping our Nation: An Economic Analysis of Canada's Consulting Engineers*, (Vancouver: Fraser Institute, 1989).

HARRIS, R. G., "Applied general equilibrium analysis of small open economies with scale economies and imperfect competition," *American Economic Review* 74 (1984):1016-33.

HARRIS, R. G. and D. Cox, *Trade, Industrial Policy and Canadian Manufacturing* (Toronto: University of Toronto Press, 1984).

HELPMAN, Elhanan, "International trade in the presence of product differentiation, economies of scale and monopolistic competition," *Journal of International Economics* 11 (1981):304-40.

HELPMAN, Elhanan and Paul R. Krugman, *Market Structure and Foreign Trade* (Cambridge: MIT Press, 1985).

_____, *Trade Policy and Market Structure* (Cambridge: MIT Press, 1989).

HOOPER, Peter and Catherine L. Mann, "The U.S. external deficit: Its causes and persistence," International Finance Discussion Papers 316, Washington, DC, 1987.

HORSTMANN, Ignatius and James R. Markusen, "Up the average cost curve: Inefficient entry and the new protectionism," *Journal of International Economics* 20 (1986):225-48.

_____, "Endogenous market structures in international trade," *Journal of International Economics*, forthcoming.

JORGENSON, D. W. and Z Griliches, "The explanation of productivity change," *The Review of Economic Studies* 34(3):99 (July 1967):249-83.

KATZ, Lawrence F. and Lawrence H. Summers, "Can interindustry wage differentials justify strategic trade policy?" in *Trade Policies for International Competitiveness*, ed. Robert C. Feenstra (Chicago: University of Chicago Press, 1989), pp. 85-116.

KEMP, Murray C., *The Pure Theory of International Trade and Investment*, (Englewood Cliffs NJ: Prentice Hall, 1969).

KRAVIS, Irving B. and Robert E. Lipsey, "Technological characteristics of industries and the competitiveness of the U.S. and its multinational firms," National Bureau of Economic Research Working Paper No. 2933, April 1989.

KRUGMAN, Paul, "Trade, accumulation, and uneven development," *Journal of Development Economics* 8 (1981):149-61.

_____, "Import protection as export promotion: international competition in the presence of oligopoly and economies of scale," in *Monopolistic Competition and International Trade*, ed. H. Kierzkowski (London: Oxford University Press, 1984).

_____, "Pricing to market when the exchange rate changes," in *Real-Financial Linkages among Open Economies*, eds. Sven W. Arndt and J. David Richardson, (Cambridge: MIT Press, 1987), pp. 49-70.

_____, "Differences in income elasticities and trends in real exchange rates," *European Economic Review* 33 (May 1989):1031-46.

_____, "Increasing returns, imperfect competition, and international trade," *Journal of Intrnational Economics* 9 (1969):469-79.

LANCASTER, Kelvin, "Intra-industry trade under perfect monopolistic competition," *Journal of International Economics* 10 (1980):151-75.

LEAMER, Edward E., *Sources of International Comparative Advantage*, (Cambridge: MIT Press, 1984).

LEVIN, Richard C., "Appropriability, R&D spending and Technological performance," *AEA Papers and Proceedings* 78:2 (May 1988):424-28.

LEVIN, Richard C. and Peter C. Reiss, "Cost-reducing and demand-creating R&D with spillovers," National Bureau of Economic Research Working Paper No. 2876, March 1989.

LICHTENBERG, Frank R. and Donald Siegel, "The impact of R&D investment on productivity — new evidence using linked R&D-LRD data," National Bureau of Economic Research Working Paper No. 2901, March 1989.

LIPSEY, Richard G., "Global imbalances and American trade policy," *Atlantic Economic Journal* 41 (June 1988):1-11.

_____, "Growth, erosion and restructuring of the multilateral trading system," Working Paper for Economic Growth and Policy Program, Canadian Institute for Advanced Research, Simon Fraser University, January 1990.

LIPSEY, Richard G. and Wendy Dobson, eds. *Shaping Comparative Advantage*, C. D. Howe Institute, Policy Study No. 2, 1987.

LIPSEY, Richard G. and Murray G. Smith, *Global Imbalances and U.S. Policy Responses: A Canadian Perspective*, CAC 54, (Toronto: C. D. Howe Institute [Canada] and Washington, DC: National Planning Association [USA], 1987).

LIPSEY, Robert E., "The internalization of production," National Bureau of Economic Research Working Paper No. 2923, April 1989.

LODH, Bimal, "Estimation of comparative advantage across countries: theory and practice (A summary of findings)," Economic Council of Canada, mimeo, March 1990.

LUCAS, Robert E. Jr., "On the mechanics of uneven development," *Journal of Monetary Economics* 22 (1989):3-24.

MAGUN, Sunder and Someshwar Rao, "The competitive position of Canada in high-technology trade," Economic Council of Canada, mimeo, 1989.

MANN, Catherine L., "Prices, profit margins, and exchange rates," *Federal Reserve Bulletin* 72 (1986):366-79.

_____, "The effects of exchange rate trends and volatility on export prices: Industry examples from Japan, Germany, and the United States," *Weltwirtschaftliches Archiv* 125 (1989):586-618.

MARKUSEN, James R., "Trade and the gains from trade with imperfect competition," *Journal of International Economics* 11 (1981):531-51.

_____, "Factor movements and commodity trade as complements," *Journal of International Economics* 13 (1983):341-56.

_____, "Multinationals, multi-plant economies, and the gains from trade," *Journal of International Economics* 14 (1984):205-26, reprinted in *International Trade: Selected Readings* (second edition), ed. Jagdish Bhagwati (Cambridge: MIT Press, 1988).

_____, "Canadian gains from trade in the presence of scale economies and imperfect competition," *Canada-United States Free Trade*, Volume II of the *Report* of the Royal Commission on the Economic Union and Development Prospects for Canada (Ottawa: Supply and Services Canada, 1985).

_____, *U.S. Canada Free Trade: Effects on Welfare and Sectoral Output/Employment Levels in the Short and Long Run*, (Washington: U.S. Department of Labor, 1987).

_____, "Production, trade and migration with differentiated, skilled workers," *Canadian Journal of Economics* 21 (1988):85-95.

_____, "Trade in producer services and in other specialized intermediate inputs," *American Economic Review* 79 (1989):85-95.

_____, "Micro-foundtions of external economies," *Canadian Journal of Economics* 23, forthcoming (1990a).

_____, "Derationalizing tariffs with specialized intermediate inputs and differentiated final goods," *Journal of International Economics*, forthcoming (1990b).

_____, "First mover advantages, blockaded entry, and the economics of uneven development,: in *International Trade and Trade Policy*, eds. Elhanan Helpman and Assaf Razin (Cambridge: MIT Press, 1990c).

MARKUSEN, James R. and Randy Wigle, "Nash equilibrium tariffs for the U.S. and Canada: The roles of country size, scale economies, and capital mobility," *Journal of Political Economy* 97 (1989):368-86.

MARSTON, Richard C., "Real exchange rates and productivity growth in the United States and Japan,: in *Real-Financial Linkages among Open Economies,* eds. Sven W. Arndt and J. David Richardson (Cambridge: MIT Press, 1987), pp. 71-96.

MASKUS, Keith E., "A test of the Heckscher-Ohlin-Vanek theorem: The Leontief commonplace," *Journal of International Economics* 19

(1985):201-12.

_____, "Comparing international trade data and product and national characteristics data for the analysis of trade models," Occasional Papers in International Economics, No. 1, Carl McGuire Center for International Studies, University of Colorado at Boulder, October 1989.

McFETRIDGE, D. G., "Notes for presentation to CIAR economic growth and policy project conference," mimeo, Vancouver, BC, January 26-27, 1990.

McFETRIDGE, Donald G. and Douglas A. Smith, *The Economics of Vertical Disintegration*, (Vancouver: Fraser Institute, 1988).

MELVIN, James R., "Increasing returns to scale as a determinant of trade," *Canadian Journal of Economics* 2 (1969):389-402.

MORRISON, Cathering J., "Markups in U.S. and Japanese manufacturing: A short run econometric analysis," National Bureau of Economic Research Working Paper No. 2799, December 1988.

_____, "Unraveling the productivity growth slowdown in the U.S., Canada and Japan: The effects of subequilibrium, scale economies and markups," National Bureau of Economic Research Working Paper No. 2993, June 1989.

MUSZYNSKI, Leon and David A. Wolfe, "New technology and training: Lessons from abroad," *Canadian Public Policy* 40:3 (1989):245-64.

OBSTFELD, Maurice, "How integrated are world capital markets? Some new tests," in *Debt Stabilization and Development: Essays in Memory of Carlos Diaz-Alejandro*, eds. G. Calvo, et al, (New York: Harper & Row, 1989) pp. 134-55.

POLESE, M. and R. Verreault, "Trade in information-based services: How and why regions develop export advantages," *Canadian Public Policy* 15 (1989):376-86.

RICHARDSON, J. David, "Figures, tables and references for Empirical research on trade liberalization with imperfect competition: A survey," National Bureau of Economic Research Working Paper No. 2883a, March 1989.

ROMER, Paul M., "Increasing returns and long-run growth," *Journal of Political Economy* 94 (1986):1002-38.

_____, "Growth based on increasing returns due to specialization," *American Economic Review* 77 (1987):56-62.

_____, "Human capital and growth: Theory and evidence," National Bureau of Economic Research Working Paper No. 3173, November 1989.

SHAKED, A. and J. Sutton, "Natural oligopolies and international trade," in *Monopolistic Competition and International Trade,* ed. H. Kierzkowski (London: Oxford University Press, 1984).

SOLOW, Robert M., "Technical change and the aggregate production function," *Review of Economic and Statistics* 39 (August 1957):312-20.

SPENCER, B. J. and J. A. Brander, "International R&D rivalry and industrial